EAGLE SCOUTS
A CENTENNIAL HISTORY

EAGLE SCOUTS
A CENTENNIAL HISTORY

Written By Robert Birkby

LONDON, NEW YORK,
MUNICH, MELBOURNE, DELHI

Author Robert Birkby
Designer Richard Czapnik
Editor Joe Staines
Senior Production Controller Verity Powell
Associate Publisher Nigel Duffield
Publishing Director Sophie Mitchell

First American Edition, 2012

Published in The United States by DK Publishing, Inc.
375 Hudson Street, New York, New York 10014
12 13 14 15 16 10 9 8 7 6 5 4 3 2
002-186415-SEP/12
Copyright © 2012

America.www.scouting.org
A cataloging-in-publication record for this book
is available from the Library of Congress
ISBN 978-0-7566-9771-6

DK books are available at special discounts for bulk purchases for sales promotions, premiums, fund-raising, or educational use. For details, contact: DK Publishing Special Markets, 375 Hudson Street, New York, NY 10014 or SpecialSales@dk.com

Printed and bound in China by Toppan

Discover more at
WWW.DK.COM

FOR MORE INFORMATION ABOUT THE BOY SCOUTS OF AMERICA OR ITS
PROGRAMS, VISIT **WWW.SCOUTING.ORG**

TO LEARN MORE ABOUT THE NATIONAL SCOUTING MUSEUM, HOME OF THE
FIRST EAGLE SCOUT AWARD AND MANY OTHER BSA ARTIFACTS, VISIT
WWW.NATIONALSCOUTINGMUSEUM.ORG

Contents

CHAPTER 1
What is an Eagle Scout?

CHAPTER 2
Trail to Eagle

CHAPTER 3
Insignia and Emblems

CHAPTER 4
Eagle Scout Service

Foreword by Robert J. Mazzuca

Coming from a family of eight children with an Italian immigrant father, we didn't have a lot of money when I was growing up. What we did have was a 1949 Studebaker truck. Shortly after I joined Scouting, my Scoutmaster asked my dad if he could use that truck to take our troop's equipment to summer camp. On that trip I saw my dad transform right before my eyes (although I didn't recognize it at the time). He got his first taste of true American volunteerism. He connected with what was going on around him. And he saw the true magic of Scouting.

Fast forward to the night in 1963 that he and my mom pinned my Eagle badge to my chest. In his eyes, I saw a pride and a sense of accomplishment that can only be described as the fulfillment of the American Dream through the eyes of an immigrant. When I left for college two years later, the first of his children to do so, my dad bid me farewell with a crumpled 20 dollar bill and the words, "Remember, son, you are an Eagle Scout."

This year, we celebrate the centennial of the Eagle Scout Award, and the more than two million young men who have earned the Boy Scouts of America's highest rank. We have seen record numbers of Eagle Scouts in recent years, averaging around 50,000 annually. But behind the facts and figures, dates and anniversaries, it is important to remember what being an Eagle Scout actually means, and how this program sets the agenda for building our future leaders.

In 100 years, we have seen Eagle Scouts make their marks on history, from walking on the Moon and working behind the desk in the Oval Office to running the bases in the major leagues. While we're proud to claim some truly great men among our ranks, we're even more proud that Eagle Scouts become wonderful husbands, fathers, and citizens—everyday stand-up guys, in every walk of life.

Recently, independent research conducted by Baylor University found that Eagle Scouts reported closer relationships with family and friends, and a greater likelihood to volunteer and give to charity than those uninvolved in Scouting. It also found that they're more goal-oriented, have better planning and preparation skills, and are more likely to sit in a leadership position. This research validates for the world something we've known for years. Eagle Scouts are special.

The findings really aren't surprising when you consider everything that goes into achieving the rank. Scouts put themselves to the test. Each one must earn 21 life skills merit badges and complete an extensive, self-directed service project that he plans, organizes, leads, and manages. Those projects average 130 hours each, representing almost 6.7 million hours of community service in 2011 alone. Earning the Eagle Scout Award requires leadership, service, character, personal fitness, outdoor skills, and a heck of a lot of elbow grease. Fewer than 5 percent of Boy Scouts make Eagle. The ones that do are exceptional.

Take, for example, 15-year-old Eagle Scout Spencer Zimmerman. When Spencer learned that his friend Dayton—a young man with cerebral palsy—liked to feel the wind in his face, he invited him to compete in a triathlon. To help him achieve the impossible, Spencer pulled, pushed, and carried Dayton through a 500-meter swim, 3.2-mile run, and 12-mile bike ride. This story of friendship, dedication, and sheer physical toughness is made even more meaningful by the attitudes of both of these young men. Spencer gives full credit for completing the race to Dayton. He says that he just loaned his legs.

I'm incredibly proud to belong to an esteemed group that includes people like Spencer Zimmerman. The Eagle badge is a mark of distinction. Once earned, it is worn for life. However, while being an Eagle Scout is an accomplishment to be proud of, it is also a responsibility—to live and lead with integrity.

I know the pride I felt when my parents pinned my Eagle Scout badge to my chest long ago. And I feel good knowing that the values that were important then are just as important today, and growing. As they progress through life, I would encourage every young man that earns the rank to take a piece of advice from my dad. Always remember, you are an Eagle Scout.

Robert J. Mazzuca
Chief Scout Executive
Boy Scouts of America
September 2007–August 2012

What is an Eagle Scout?

WHAT IS AN EAGLE SCOUT?
"Any first class scout qualifying for twenty-one merit badges will be entitled to wear the highest scout merit badge. This is an eagle's head in silver, and represents the all-round perfect scout."

1911 *Boy Scout Handbook*, p. 43

Awards and gifts at an Eagle Scout Court of Honor.

Eagle Scouts in Action

Boys join Scouting in search of adventure. They want to hike and camp with their friends. They can't wait to explore all the activities Boy Scouts get to do. The progression through the ranks from Tenderfoot to Eagle is an unfolding of possibilities that encourages Scouts to move forward. The more they learn and do, the more exciting they find the challenges.

Those who continue all the way to Eagle have gained years of experience as leaders and learners. They have equipped themselves with Scouting skills and values they can use wherever they go. Emergency preparedness and environmental responsibility have become second nature to them.

Eagle Scouts know they wouldn't trade their BSA experiences for anything. Best of all, they are just the beginning of a lifetime of great adventures to come.

◄ SOUNDING THE CHALLENGE

For more than a century, Eagle Scouts have responded to the call of the BSA by lacing up their hiking boots, swinging their packs onto their shoulders, and setting out to discover the world.

▼ ROCK CLIMBING

Rock climbing is just one of many exciting sports open to Eagle Scouts. It demands fitness, concentration, and problem solving skills.

◄ **HIGH SEAS ADVENTURES**
With one hand for the ship and one hand for themselves, Sea Scouts embark on voyages that can lead to the Eagle pin or to Quartermaster, Sea Scouting's highest rank.

TRAIL TO THE FUTURE ►
Scouting is a game with a purpose. The game is full of adventure and the joy of sharing great times with fellow Scouts. The purpose is to help Scouts become confident adults prepared for the future. That's as true for the newest Tenderfoot as it is for the most seasoned Eagle in a troop.

Why Become an Eagle Scout?

Eagle Scouts of every age know that "Once an Eagle, always an Eagle." Whether they have held that rank for a day or for decades, they realize that reaching Scouting's highest rank has prepared each of them for a future open to possibilities, opportunities, and continuing adventures.

Becoming an Eagle Scout changes a young man. He gains experience as a problem solver and as someone willing to step up and do his part. By serving in positions of responsibility in his troop, he has become a proven leader. He knows how to take charge during meetings, motivate people, and make things happen.

An Eagle Scout has trained himself to act effectively in times of emergency, and be a positive influence in his family, his community, and his nation. From organizing service projects to following the Trail to Eagle, he has discovered ways to set goals, figured out the steps to achieve them, and learned how to transform a vision of the future into the reality of the present.

Scouting brings boys together with adult leaders who live by the principles of the Scout Oath and Law. Those values become woven into an Eagle Scout's character, too, guiding his decisions now and in the years to come.

Leaders guiding and encouraging a Scout are eager to acknowledge his accomplishments, especially when he completes the requirements for Eagle. The Boy Scouts of America acknowledges success on the Trail to Eagle as an achievement worthy of celebration.

Many people outside of Scouting take notice when they discover someone is an Eagle. They might not know exactly how he earned that distinction, but they realize that standing before them is a trustworthy man who is prepared to do his best. That's a reputation an Eagle will be glad to carry with him for the rest of his life.

◄ **SPEAKING OUT**
Anthony Thomas, the two millionth Eagle Scout, addresses the crowd at the National Scout Jamboree in 2010. Speaking in public is a valuable skill that Scouts are encouraged to master. By the time they reach the Eagle rank, they have stepped before their patrols and troops many times. They have made presentations to adults, too, in troop planning sessions and during boards of review.

NAVIGATING ►
There is much truth in the belief that Eagle Scouts can find their way. With maps, compasses, and Global Positioning System (GPS) receivers, they can plot a course to reach any destination. The Scout Oath and Law are equally reliable tools of navigation, guiding scouts to make good choices throughout their lives.

▲ OVAL OFFICE WELCOME

Eagle Scouts are recognized by many, including the President of the United States. Each year, at least one Eagle joins a BSA contingent traveling to Washington, DC, to present the Report to the Nation. It's a current overview of Scouting and of the BSA's continuing commitment to prepare young people to be honorable citizens.

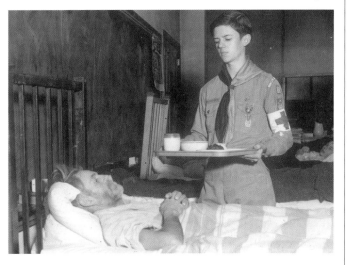

▲ SERVICE

An Eagle pin is an important milestone in a young man's life. It represents years of effort on his part, and qualities of character that he will carry with him in the years to come. One of those values is being of service to others. All Scouts "Do a Good Turn Daily." Eagles have also organized and completed significant projects that help them realize that there are few limits to what they can accomplish.

How It All Began

In 1900, British army officer Robert Baden-Powell became a national hero following his defense of the besieged town of Mafeking during Britain's war against the Boers in South Africa. When he returned to England a few years later, he discovered that his short military manual, *Aids to Scouting for NCOs and Men*, had become an unexpected success with young people.

Wanting to do something to help youngsters find greater direction in their lives, Baden-Powell threw himself into outlining a program for boys that would use outdoor activities to develop character and citizenship. He rewrote his earlier book as *Scouting for Boys: A Handbook of Instruction for Good Citizenship Through Woodcraft*. In addition to the skills in the original manual, he also included activities and games devised by American youth leader Ernest Thompson Seton. The new book presented boys with the framework of an organization that would become the worldwide Scouting movement.

Much of what Baden-Powell proposed is recognizable today as the heart of Scouting. Boys wore broad-brimmed hats and khaki uniforms. They did good turns for others. Patrols formed the basic building blocks of Scout troops, and the troops were led by scoutmasters. Members pledged themselves to uphold the principles of a Scout law and oath. Passing certain tests allowed a Scout to wear a First Class emblem. If he completed other requirements, he could become a King's Scout, the highest rank of the British Scout Association. Each King's Scout received an embroidered emblem to sew on his uniform. He was also given a royal certificate signed by the king that include this message:

"As a King's Scout you have prepared yourself for service to God and your fellow men, and have shown yourself a worthy member of the great SCOUT BROTHERHOOD. I wish you Godspeed on your journey through life; may it prove for you a joyous adventure."

The King's Scout recognition set the precedent for encouraging and celebrating Scouting achievement with an award of special merit. Several years later, the Boy Scouts of America began granting the Eagle Scout medal to members who reached the BSA's highest rank. It incorporated the spirit and high honor of the King's Scout Award, but like all of Scouting in the United States, the eagle was better suited to the character of American boys and to the nation where Scouting was beginning to thrive.

◀ **CHIEF SCOUT**
Through the Scout Oath and Law, Robert Baden-Powell instilled the Scout movement with strong values. He was a driving force in launching Scouting in Britain and became known as the Chief Scout of the World.

SKETCHES ▲
Baden-Powell was a talented artist. His ability to illustrate books and magazine articles, as in this drawing for *Scouting for Boys*, helped promote the excitement and ideals of early Scouting.

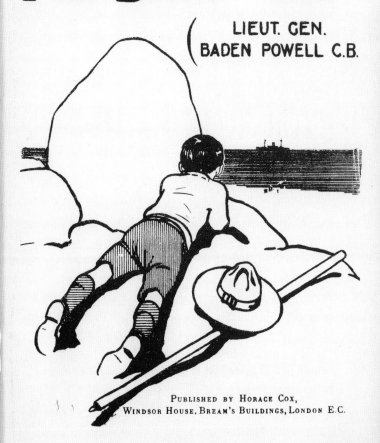

Part I.   Price 4d. net

SCOUTING FOR BOYS BY B-P

(LIEUT. GEN.
BADEN POWELL C.B.

PUBLISHED BY HORACE COX,
WINDSOR HOUSE, BREAM'S BUILDINGS, LONDON E.C.

▲ A SCOUT IS CHEERFUL

Cheerful optimism guided Robert Baden-Powell as he brought Scouting to young people. His first version of the Scout Law included number eight—"A SCOUT SMILES AND WHISTLES under all circumstances." Near the end of his life he wrote, "The most worth-while thing is to try to put happiness into the lives of others."

▲ SCOUTING FOR BOYS

Baden-Powell filled his 1908 book, *Scouting for Boys* with stories of adventure and instructions for enjoying life in the outdoors. He also did the pen and ink sketches that appeared inside the book and on the cover. It was an instant best-seller. The new British Scout organization encouraged the boys who bought it to try the activities they had been reading about.

TESTING THE SCHEME ▶

Camping on Brownsea Island, just off the south coast of England, enabled Baden-Powell to try out some of his ideas for a Scout organization. In August 1907, he and other adult leaders joined 22 boys on an eight day encampment. Baden-Powell guided them as they practiced woodcraft skills. During evening campfires he shared stories of his life and talked of chivalry, honor, and responsibility.

Scouting Comes to America

As the Scout movement gained momentum in Britain, civic leaders in the United States realized that boys on their side of the Atlantic Ocean were ready for a Scouting program, too. They also knew that while their organization would owe much to the British model, it would be even more influenced by a robust vision of America itself.

Many boys in the United States knew about pioneers, frontiersmen, Indians, and settlers. Their imaginations were fired by America's wide open spaces. "From sea to shining sea" meant a vast expanse of prairies, mountains, and forests, much of it still wild country. The new Boy Scouts of America sought to channel boys' enthusiasm into programs that made it possible for them to have real outdoor adventures and live by the Scout Oath and Law.

Among those involved in the birth of the Boy Scouts of America were two men with strong wilderness sensibilities. Ernest Thompson Seton and Daniel Carter Beard were authors and artists who had started youth organizations of their own. Beard's group, The Sons of Daniel Boone, celebrated the skills and exploits of American pioneers. Seton based The League of Woodcraft Indians on the lore of Native Americans. Both men encouraged boys to hike, camp, and become self-sufficient.

Seton shared his writings with Robert Baden-Powell, who incorporated many of Seton's ideas into his book, *Scouting for Boys*. A few years later, Seton's original edition of the *Boy Scout Handbook* borrowed concepts from Baden-Powell to develop the framework of Scout patrols and troops. Beard added some of his own knowledge of woodcraft skills. Other founders developed the administrative structure of the new organization and built the BSA's system for earning badges and gaining ranks.

Considering how quickly it all came together, those figuring out Scouting for American boys managed to get almost everything right. For example, they took the ten points of Baden-Powell's Scout Law, added two more, then streamlined the twelve down to one word each. Unchanged for more than a century, the Scout Law today is identical to that recited by the first Scouts long ago.

With lofty ideals, an embrace of adventure, and the energy of a nation still discovering itself, the BSA needed a highest rank worthy of the organization's great intent. They charted a pathway of challenge and achievement leading to an award they named for that most recognizable of U.S. symbols, the American eagle.

◄ **ERNEST THOMPSON SETON**
A best-selling author and illustrator of books about wildlife, Seton brought his love of the outdoors to the new Boy Scouts of America. He believed that a key responsibility of the BSA would be to introduce boys to nature.

BIRCH BARK ROLL ▶
Filled with illustrated descriptions of wild animals and plants, Seton's book also described how to build a waterproof camp shelter, light a fire without matches, and predict weather by looking at clouds. Baden-Powell included games from *The Birch Bark Roll* in his own book, *Scouting for Boys*.

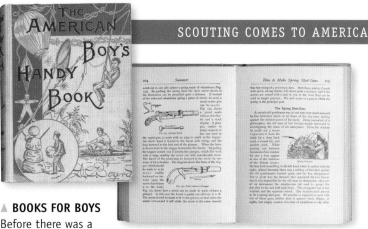

BOOKS FOR BOYS

Before there was a
Boy Scout Handbook,
manuals showing boys how to have fun outdoors were clues
that America was ready for Scouting. *The American Boy's Handy
Book* by Daniel Beard was published in 1882.

DANIEL CARTER BEARD

"Uncle Dan" was a fixture in the BSA for more than 30 years. His
writings and drawings in *Boys' Life* magazine encouraged boys to
build everything from sleds and war kites to teepees and log
cabins. Dressed in his trademark buckskin jacket and leggings, he
emphasized the correct use and care of pocketknives, axes, saws,
and other working tools.
He is the only person to
have been given the
Gold Eagle Badge, the
forerunner of the
Distinguished Eagle
Scout Award.

SILVER BAY CAMP

Boy Scouts were going camping even before they had uniforms. This group
tenting near Lake George in upstate New York typified the power of outdoor
adventure as an essential component of Scouting in America.

Charting the Route to Eagle

It would be several years after the founding of the Boy Scouts of America in February of 1910 before any Scouts advanced far enough to reach the organization's highest rank. It would also take time for Scouting's originators to figure out exactly what that award would be and how members would get there.

Early BSA literature explained that Scouts could complete requirements to earn the ranks of Tenderfoot, Second Class, and First Class. Those were distinctions borrowed from Robert Baden-Powell's book, *Scouting for Boys,* that had laid the foundations for Scouting in England. Beyond First Class, the BSA envisioned Scouts expanding their skills by passing requirements for any of 14 "badges of merit"— Ambulance, Clerk, Cyclist, Electrician, Fireman, Gardener, Horseman, Pioneer, Marksman, Master-at-Arms, Musician, Signaller, Seaman, and Stalker. A First Class Scout who earned them all would be given the Silver Wolf Award, another idea borrowed from Baden-Powell. In fact, neither the "badges of merit" nor the Silver Wolf pin were ever produced.

A year later, the 1911 edition of the *Boy Scout Handbook* introduced 57 "merit badges" in subjects ranging from Agriculture to Taxidermy.

First Class Scouts who earned the merit badges for First Aid, Athletics, Life-Saving, Personal Health, and Public Health could wear the Life Scout Award. A Life Scout who earned those five badges and five more would be given the Star Scout emblem. (Life and Star ranks would switch names in 1924.)

The *Boy Scout Handbook* devoted just two sentences to what would become Scouting's highest earned award. "Any first-class scout qualifying for twenty-one merit badges will be entitled to wear the highest scout merit badge. This is an eagle's head in silver, and represents the all-round perfect scout." The silver wolf of Baden-Powell had become an American eagle.

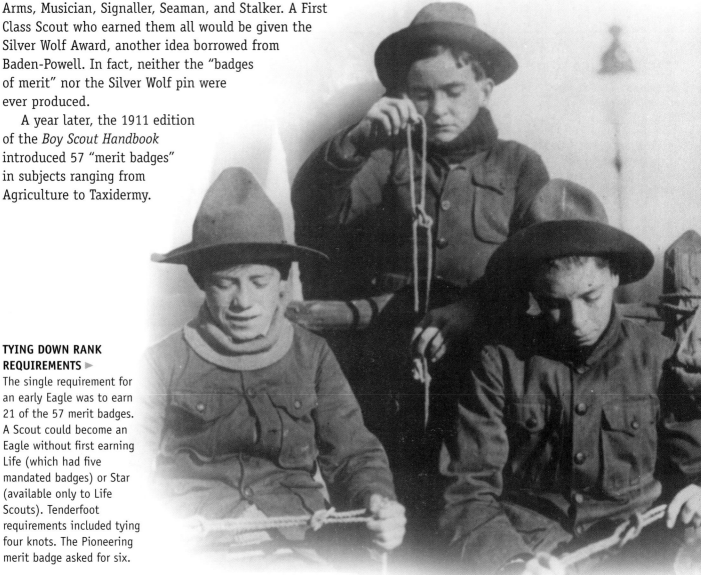

TYING DOWN RANK REQUIREMENTS ▷
The single requirement for an early Eagle was to earn 21 of the 57 merit badges. A Scout could become an Eagle without first earning Life (which had five mandated badges) or Star (available only to Life Scouts). Tenderfoot requirements included tying four knots. The Pioneering merit badge asked for six.

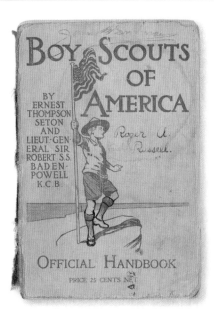

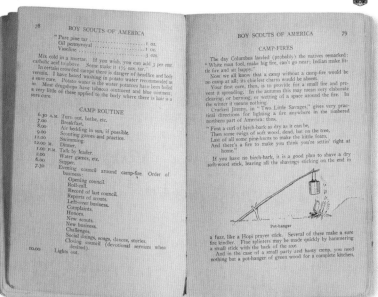

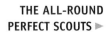

◄ THE EAGLE PIN THAT NEVER WAS

The 1911 handbook described the Eagle Scout Award as "an eagle's head in silver" even though the accompanying sketch showed the profile of an eagle in flight. By the time the first Eagle received his pin, the medal had changed again to the iconic form still recognized today.

▲ THE "ORIGINAL" HANDBOOK

The 1910 "original edition" *Boy Scout Handbook* blended much of Baden-Powell's *Scouting for Boys* with writings by Ernest Thompson Seton and others. Intended to serve as the BSA manual only until a fully American version could be completed, it described the ranks of Tenderfoot, Second Class, and First Class, but made no mention of Eagle.

THE ALL-ROUND PERFECT SCOUTS ►

In the rush to develop programs, early BSA administrators tried a variety of approaches for advancement and the awards it should produce. Something never in doubt, though, was that Scouting's highest earned badge would recognize the best that boys could be.

The First Eagle Scout

On August 21, 1912, Arthur Eldred of Rockville Center, New York, became the first Eagle Scout. "That the distinction is unusual is shown by the fact that the National Court of Honor of the Boy Scouts of America have awarded in one year only 141 merit badges to about 50 different boys," *Boys' Life* magazine reported. The article also called Arthur "a sturdy, well-built, keen-eyed little fellow, and his Scoutmaster commends him highly."

Growing up in Oceanside, New York, Arthur joined Troop 1 in nearby Rockville Center, where his brother was the Scoutmaster. Troop highlights included assembling in New York City to greet the ship bringing Robert Baden-Powell to America. As he reviewed the troop, the founder of the Scouting movement shook hands with Arthur Eldred and talked with him about the merit badges sewn on his sleeve and the First Class pin on his hat.

Later that year, Arthur earned his 21st merit badge and appeared at the National Council offices to be reviewed before being declared the first Eagle. That same month, Eldred rescued a fellow Scout, Melvin Daly, from drowning, a

heroic action the BSA recognized by giving Arthur the Honor Medal for saving a life at risk to his own.

Arthur Eldred went on to study agriculture at Cornell University, graduating in 1916. He served aboard a U.S. Navy submarine chaser during World War I, before embarking on a successful career as an agricultural agent and then as a transportation expert for the railroad industry.

FIRST OF TWO MILLION ▶
Arthur Eldred's Eagle Scout pin is on display alongside his merit badges at the National Scouting Museum in Irving, Texas.

PROVING HIS WORTH
The BSA's National Court of Honor convened to review Arthur Eldred on his achievements before granting him the first Eagle Scout Award. In a scene similar to that shown in this sketch from the 1914 *Boy Scout Handbook*, Eldred was questioned by Scouting founders Ernest Thompson Seton, Daniel Carter Beard, and James E. West.

ELDRED'S MERIT BADGES ▶
The first Eagle Scout's 21 badges were (from upper left) Personal Fitness, Plumbing, Gardening, Cooking, Painting, Swimming, Civics, Lifesaving, Public Health, Cycling, Pathfinding, Interpreting, Electricity, Dairying, First Aid to Animals, Chemistry, Business, and Handicraft, Firemanship, Horsemanship, and Poultry Farming.

CONTINUING THE LEGACY
Arthur Eldred stayed active in Scouting as a troop committeeman and as an examiner on boards of review. He also encouraged others to pursue the Eagle Scout Award, including his son Willard, shown in 1944 receiving his Eagle pin from a BSA executive while his father looked on.

FOURTH GENERATION EAGLE
Two of Arthur Eldred's grandsons, James Hudson III and Willard Eldred, became Eagle Scouts. In 2010, during the BSA's centennial year and the 98th anniversary of the first Eagle Scout Award, Arthur Eldred's great-grandson Tennessee Abbott (pictured to the right of a celebratory cake) received his Eagle Scout pin.

Other Early Eagle Scouts

Scouting celebrates Arthur Eldred of Rockville Center, New York, as the first Eagle Scout. Right behind him was Earl Marx, a fellow from Jacksonville, Florida. "These two Scouts, one from the North and one from the South, stand alone among their 400,000 comrades as being the only Scouts who have won 21 merit badges," noted an August, 1912, *Boys' Life* magazine article. "However, there are others in the race as Scout Abner H. Parker, of Bedford, Massachusetts, and Scout Bruce K. Brown of Wilmette, Illinois, have each won 12 badges. There will be a great race between these two Scouts for the honor of winning the third Eagle badge."

In fact, that badge went to Roy Young of St. Paul, Minnesota. He was probably the first to earn 21 merit badges, but the board of review that considered his candidacy convened after those for Arthur Eldred and Earl Marx. The BSA's third Eagle Scout, Roy was described by the secretary of the National Court of Honor as "a typical wide-awake Scout, alive to every opportunity, prepared for any emergency. We are proud to list him with Eldred and Marx."

Scouts and leaders in West Shokan, New York, earned Eagle medals four through eight. Rounding out the BSA's first dozen Eagles were:

9th Francis R. Edwards of Jacksonville, Florida

10th Scoutmaster D. Mac O. Little of Morristown, New Jersey

11th Scout Commissioner J. Van Buren Mitchell of Morristown, New Jersey

12th William Bennett of Cohoes, New York

▲ **THE WEST SHOKAN FIVE**
The fourth through eighth Eagle pins went to members of a troop in West Shokan, New York. Pictured from left, they were Jack S. Langthorn, Robert Pleasants, Sidney Clapp, and brothers Bertram and Leon Van Vliet. In those days, adults could earn the Eagle Scout Award, and Scoutmaster Clapp was the first to do so.

THEODORE GATZ, JR. ▶
Labeled "Silver Eagle Scout," this 1913 photograph of Theodore Gatz, Jr., was mistakenly identified in 1980s and 90s BSA literature as first Eagle Scout Arthur Eldred. In a 2003 letter to *Scouting* magazine, Mr. Eldred's son Willard corrected the error.

Fifty years later, Earl Marx recalled that "Winning merit badges was no easier then than now; you had to know the subject, prove you knew it, and demonstrate often." He had been especially interested in passing the tests for the aviation merit badge. "In the aviation field—an infant at the time—a Scout needed almost as much knowledge as a pilot," Mr. Marx said. As is still true today, Scout experiences could lead to careers. Earl Marx went on to become a flight instructor and airline captain.

Asked about the most important lessons he had gained from Scouting, the BSA's second Eagle Scout gave an answer that could have come from any Eagle, whether he was number one or number two million and one. "The code I learned as a Scout is the code I live by as an adult. Pass that word along to the youth of this community, this county, this country."

COVER EAGLE ▶
The first appearance of an Eagle Scout on the cover of *Boys' Life* magazine was the July issue of 1915. The image of a senior patrol leader who had earned his Life, Star, and Eagle ranks shared the page with a note from Woodrow Wilson. "It is fine," President Wilson wrote, "to have the boys of the country organized for the purposes the Boy Scouts represent."

27

Trail to Eagle

TRAIL TO EAGLE
"The long trail to Eagle is full of opportunities for you to learn, to lead, to listen, and to teach. Along the way and throughout your life, the rewards from earning the Eagle Scout Award will be great."

1998 *Boy Scout Handbook*, p. 179

Trail to Eagle (1985) by Ted Summers.

Evolution of Eagle Scout Requirements

The requirements for earning the Eagle Scout Award have been adjusted now and then throughout Scouting's first century. Changes have often been minor, but there have been several major overhauls as the Boy Scouts of America has attempted to keep pace with changes in the needs of Scouts and in the best ways to help them prepare for the future.

The Eagle requirements of 1911 asked only that a Scout earn any 21 of the original 57 merit badges. By 1915, 11 of those badges were specified—First Aid, Physical Development, Lifesaving, Personal Health, Public Health, Cooking, Camping, Bird Study, Pathfinding, Pioneering, and Athletics. Civics came along the next year, and Scouts could earn either Athletics or Physical Development. Swimming was added a decade later, bringing to an even dozen the number of required merit badges.

By the early 1930s, a Scout also needed three months' tenure as a First Class Scout, three more as a Star Scout, and six as a Life Scout. In 1952, the BSA required that a Scout complete all requirements for Eagle by age 18. Before then, many adults had earned Eagle pins.

Complicated requirement changes of 1958 asked Eagles to earn merit badges in Camping, Swimming, Nature, Public Health, Firemanship, Cooking, Lifesaving, Personal Fitness, Safety, and First Aid. They also needed one badge from a group of conservation-oriented merit badges, three from a citizenship group, and one representing either transportation or building. The remaining five merit badges were open to the Scout's choice.

The 1972 Improved Scouting Program increased to 24 the number of merit badges required for Eagle. Only

ten were specified. Camping and Cooking were no longer needed, and Personal Fitness or Sports could be substituted for Swimming. A boy could, in theory, become an Eagle Scout without knowing much about swimming or camping.

Responding in 1979 to the unpopularity of the Improved Scouting Program, the BSA reinstituted much of the former emphasis of the Eagle requirements, including returning the number of merit badges to 21 and promoting leadership, service, and outdoor skills. With modest adjustments, those requirements are still in place today.

◄ "FOR ME TO BE AND DO"
A page from the 1945 *Boy Scout Handbook* gave Life Scouts a handy scorecard for tracking their progress toward Eagle. In addition to earning merit badges, each candidate promised that he was "Earnestly trying to develop leadership ability."

OUTLINE FOR THE FUTURE ►
The merit badges that must be earned along the Trail to Eagle have been selected over the years to insure that those who reach the BSA's highest rank have had opportunities to master skills that will serve them well—not just in the outdoors, but in all aspects of their lives.

MORE THAN AN AWARD ▼ ▶
From the days of wicker pack baskets and canvas rucksacks to today's high-tech backcountry gear, boys have thrived on the challenges offered by the BSA. The Trail to Eagle has helped them make the most of their BSA experiences and to be acknowledged for their efforts with an award recognized everywhere.

▲ **GETTING IT DONE**
Today's Eagle Scouts earn 21 merit badges, including these that are required: First Aid, Citizenship in the Community, Citizenship in the Nation, Citizenship in the World, Communications, Personal Fitness, Emergency Preparedness or Lifesaving, Environmental Science, Personal Management, Swimming or Hiking or Cycling, Camping, and Family Life.

Scout's Progress

Requirements to earn the ranks of Scouting from Tenderfoot to Eagle provide boys with challenges and opportunities to learn, to lead, and to set off on terrific adventures. A Scout plans his advancement and then progresses at his own pace from one rank to the next. The more he learns, the more he can do as a Scout. One rank flows into another, helping a Boy Scout grow in self-reliance and in his ability to be of service to others. To acknowledge and celebrate the achievement of a higher rank, the BSA grants a Scout a cloth emblem to sew on his uniform shirt and a card to carry in his wallet. Gordon Knutson of eastern Iowa's Winnebago Council kept most of his advancement cards (see below) as a record of his progress to earning Eagle Scout. His Tenderfoot card is missing (replaced here by Douglas Calliham's card) but the presence of the other five attests to the fact that Gordon's BSA beginnings launched him on the pathway to success.

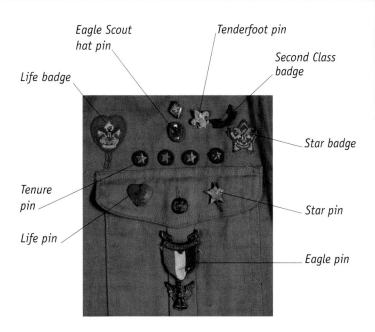

Eagle Scout hat pin · Tenderfoot pin · Second Class badge · Life badge · Star badge · Tenure pin · Star pin · Life pin · Eagle pin

PRIDE IN PROGRESS ▲
The shirt of a Scout of the 1910s or early 1920s displays his history of advancement from his first days in a troop to the acceptance of his Eagle Scout pin. Today's Scout wears just one emblem of rank at a time to represent all he has accomplished.

SCOUT __Douglas Calliham__
TROOP __392__
IS HEREBY CERTIFIED AS A
TENDERFOOT SCOUT
DATE __5/62__
Muskingum Valley __COUNCIL__
__SCOUTMASTER__

SCOUT __Gordon Knutson__
TROOP __75 Clear Lake__
IS HEREBY CERTIFIED AS A
SECOND CLASS SCOUT
DATE __2/4/52__
__WINNEBAGO__ COUNCIL
ADVANCEMENT COMMITTEE
SCOUT EXECUTIVE

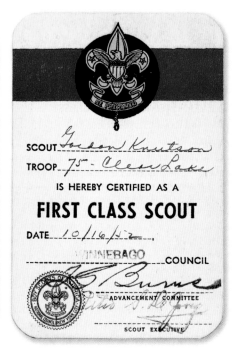

SCOUT __Gordon Knutson__
TROOP __75 Clear Lake__
IS HEREBY CERTIFIED AS A
FIRST CLASS SCOUT
DATE __10/16/52__
__WINNEBAGO__ COUNCIL
ADVANCEMENT COMMITTEE
SCOUT EXECUTIVE

TENDERFOOT ▲
To earn his first badge of rank, a boy is encouraged to jump into the adventure of Scouting by joining his patrol in planning and then going on an overnight campout. He also gains confidence by learning a bit about first aid, citizenship, knot tying, and the values of Scouting.

SECOND CLASS ▲
Second Class introduces more outdoor skills including use of fires and stoves, knives and axes, and compasses. There are more campouts and hikes, a swimming test, first aid training for "hurry cases", and more encouragement to live by the Scout Oath.

FIRST CLASS ▲
The requirements for First Class prepare a boy to take part in most of his troop's adventures. Often reached by the end of his first year as a Scout, a boy who wears the First Class patch should feel comfortable in the outdoors and clear about his responsibilities to himself and to his family, community, and troop.

Each Boy Scout can decide how fast to progress along the Trail to Eagle. Regardless of the level of his interest in advancement, he joins all other members of the BSA in using the Scout Oath and Law as guidelines for all that they do.

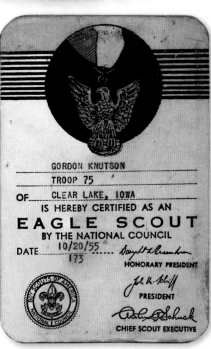

STAR ▲

In addition to earning five of the merit badges required for Eagle, Star Scouts also serve in positions of responsibility in their troops (patrol leader, historian, bugler, etc.) and conduct approved service projects of at least six hours. They have four months' tenure as First Class Scouts.

LIFE ▲

Completing the rank of Life involves six months or more as a Star Scout, earning five more merit badges (including three required for Eagle), providing leadership in the troop, and finishing another service project. Candidates must also exhibit Scout spirit by living by the Oath and Law every day.

EAGLE ▲

The final card in the set represents years of effort on the part of a Scout and a tremendous amount of learning and experience guided by rank requirements. Only a small percentage of Boy Scouts see their names on Eagle Scout cards. Most of those who do hang onto their cards for life.

Merit Badges and the Eagle Scout Award

Twenty-one. Over the years that has been the magic number of merit badges Scouts needed to earn the Eagle Scout Award (except for 1972 through 1979 when 24 were required). Of that number, anywhere from five to 16 specific badges have been required in an attempt to insure that Eagle Scouts will possess knowledge and experience that is useful and well-rounded.

Some merit badges have been short-lived. Among the first was the 1911 Invention merit badge, requiring a boy to "Invent and patent some useful article." Fewer than a dozen Scouts earned it. The Invention merit badge was discontinued in 1915, then reappeared in 2010 as Inventing. The modern version encourages designing and building the prototype of an invention (as well as learning about intellectual property and patent infringement), but without requiring a patent.

A handful of merit badges listed at the dawn of Scouting can still be earned today— Archery, Astronomy, Athletics, Camping, Cooking, Cycling, Electricity, First Aid, Forestry, Gardening, Horsemanship, Music, Painting, Photography, Pioneering, Plumbing, Public

Health, Scholarship, and Sculpture. Among them, First Aid has been the most popular merit badge with over six million earned. It is followed by Swimming, Camping, and Cooking, all required at some time for the Eagle Scout Award.

Among the recent merit badges is Robotics. It joins Inventing as one of 31 merit badges identified with the BSA's STEM program that encourages youth to explore Science, Technology, Engineering, and Math.

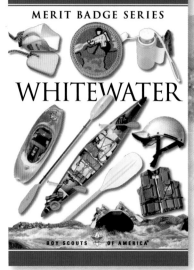

THE CHANGING FACE OF MERIT BADGES ▲ ▶
The plain khaki backgrounds of BSA merit badges of the past have given way to brightly-colored embroidery representing the excitement, adventure, and satisfaction Scouts find in earning modern merit badges. The same is true of the merit badge pamphlet Scouts can use as a guidebook for each award.

MERIT BADGES FROM A ALMOST TO Z ▶
From American Business to Woodwork, and from Backpacking to Whitewater, merit badges Scouts are earning represent a tremendous range of ways that BSA members can increase their knowledge, develop skills, and explore the world. First Aid, Citizenship in the Nation, and other required badges insure a high level of expertise among Eagle Scouts.

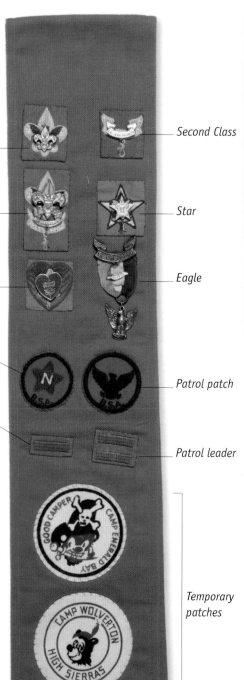

Leadership and rank insignia pins

Tenderfoot

Second Class

First Class

Star

Life

Eagle

Patrol patch

Assistant Patrol leader

Patrol patch

Patrol leader

Temporary patches

Merit badges

Service medals and leadership patches

Rank insignia patches

Temporary camp patch

SASHES AND SLEEVES ▷
Early Scouts stitched their merit badges to the right sleeves of their uniforms. Since 1924, sashes have given them room to display their merit badges and, in some cases, other BSA awards.

STORIES TOLD IN PATCHES AND PINS ▷
These vintage sashes are colorful testimonials to the Scouting careers of their owners. The dark green Explorer Scout sash features both an Eagle Scout pin and the Explorer Silver Medal.

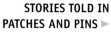

Eagle Board of Review

After he has earned 21 merit badges, completed his leadership service project, served his troop in positions of responsibility, and fulfilled all the other requirements, a Scout's final step on the Trail to Eagle is to appear before an Eagle board of review.

He will already have met with a board of review each time he finished requirements for one of the ranks of Tenderfoot through Life. Those meetings would have given adults from the troop the opportunity to understand how the Scout program could further meet the boy's interests and needs, and what the troop leadership could do to encourage him to continue moving forward.

An Eagle Scout board of review is different than those for lower ranks. It is often a more formal event involving an in-depth exchange of ideas between board members and an Eagle Scout candidate. The board will talk with him about his time in Scouting, his plans for the future, and the pathway he intends to follow. They will also ask him to speak about the values of Scouting.

In the 1920s, Scouts at Eagle boards of review in the Portland Area Council signed the following pledge:

"Realizing that a fundamental idea of Scouting is service to others, and being mindful of the worthwhile things I have learned and the assistance given me by merit badge examiners and the officers of my troop in attaining Eagle rank, I desire to record my earnest intention to aid other Scouts and Scout leaders, whenever and wherever I can, in securing all the benefits and privileges that have come to me in Scoutcraft, and always to uphold the high principles set forth in the Scout Oath and the Scout Law. Wherefore I here subscribe my signature."

Then, as now, the congratulations and handshakes at the conclusion of the board of review signaled to a young man that at that moment he had become an Eagle Scout.

▼ **DISCUSSING WHAT MATTERS**
Composed of adults associated with a candidate's troop and from the larger community, members of an Eagle Scout board of review (as in this one from 1989) are eager to hear a Scout's thoughts on his experiences with the BSA. It is a sharing of ideas that can bring him a deeper awareness of what he has accomplished and of the importance of continuing to live by the values of Scouting.

Rt. 1 Box 137 G
Atascosa, Texas 78002
6 November 1967

Mr. Terry Dimmery
110 Threadneedle
San Antonio, Texas 78227

Dear Terry:

It is my pleasure to request your presence at the Medina Valley District Eagle Board of Review to be held at the Marbach Christian Church (just off Loop 410 on Marbach Road) on Saturday, 18 November 1967.

Please be there promptly at 9:45 AM in full Scout uniform. You will receive a short briefing then, prior to reporting to the first section of the Board at 10:00 AM. This will last approximately one hour. From then until 2:00 PM we suggest that you and your family go out to dinner, do some shopping--in short, relax together. At 2:00 PM you will report to the second section of the Board. This will also take approximately one hour, after which you will be informed of our recommended action on your application. After this we will discuss a bit of your future in Scouting and the presentation of the Eagle badge. The Board will adjourn at about 3:30 PM.

I would recommend that your parents and your Scout-master accompany you, if you so desire. I look forward to meeting you then.

Yours in Scouting,

Gordon R. Knutson
Chairman, Eagle Board of Review
Medina Valley District

TAKING IT SERIOUSLY
Terry Dimmery shared a scrapbook of his Scouting experiences with a member of his Eagle Scout Board of Review. Included in the book was the letter Terry had received inviting him to appear before the board and explaining what he could expect. Today's boards of review usually do not require the full day commitment asked of Terry Dimmery, but the importance of the review has remained unchanged through the years.

Courts of Honor

In the early years of the BSA, the National Court of Honor was similar to modern boards of review that insure a Scout has completed the requirements for a higher rank. The 1914 *Boy Scout Handbook* described it this way:

"The National Court of Honor consists of citizens of the United States of sterling personal character and notable achievement in those lines of activity which are represented by the various merit badges awarded by the Boy Scouts of America, whose accomplishments will serve to inspire proper motives and ambition in the Boy Scouts."

Much of that description applies to Eagle Scouts themselves—sterling character, notable achievement, and inspiration. These are qualities worthy of notice. Eagle Scout courts of honor celebrate all that Scouts have accomplished in reaching the lofty destination at the end of the Trail to Eagle.

◄ COMMUNITY WELCOME
Public officials, religious mentors, and Scout leaders attend courts of honor to offer their heartfelt support. They also encourage new Eagle Scouts to rely on the values of Scouting for guidance throughout their lifetimes.

A GREAT MOMENT ►
Every Eagle Scout court of honor recognizes a Scout in ways that will stay with him for the rest of his life. In his 1965 painting, artist Norman Rockwell captured the deep meaning of the presentation of an Eagle Scout pin.

BROTHER EAGLES ►
Highlighting friendships forged through Scouting, courts of honor acknowledge the bonds shared by Eagle Scouts of all ages and locations.

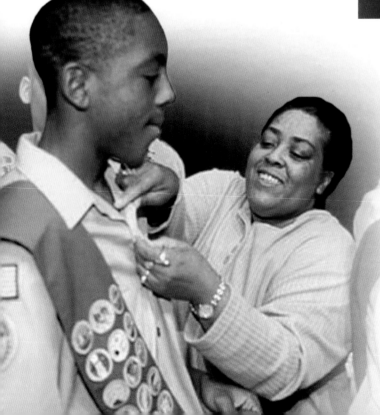

SURPRISE VISIT ►
In 1950, Doug Keppler's father asked Roy Rogers to attend his son's court of honor. The cowboy singer and movie star happily accepted the invitation and presented a giant Eagle emblem to Doug (left) and fellow Eagle Warren Stevenson.

◄ A MOTHER'S PRIDE
An Eagle court of honor is an opportunity for a family to celebrate a Scout's success, and it's a moment for him to thank relatives, neighbors, his community, and his troop for their support.

Venturing Eagles

BSA programs appealing to young adults began when Sea Scouting came to America from Britain in 1912. Rovers, Explorers, and Air Scouts appeared in the 1930s and 40s, and were unified with Sea Scouting in 1949 to form the BSA's Exploring division. Today's Venturing program, an outgrowth of Exploring, was established in 1998.

Venturing encourages members to become responsible and caring adults. The Silver Award, Venturing's ultimate medal, recognizes achievement along a pathway of personal development, leadership, service, and skills achievement. Male Venturers and Sea Scouts who have attained the First Class rank in a Boy Scout troop may also continue to progress toward the Eagle Scout Award until their eighteenth birthdays.

▲ OPPORTUNITIES FOR ALL
Venturing is coeducational. Young men and women join together in the healthy pursuit of adventure, service, learning, and Scouting values. Chosen, planned, and carried out by its members, Venturing's crew activities can be as wide-ranging as climbing mountains, sailing in Caribbean waters, and helping children at a neighborhood school learn to read.

◀ THE SILVER AWARD
The Silver Award can be earned by a Venturer until his or her twenty-first birthday.

◀▲ EXPLORERS AND AIR SCOUTS
Before the Venturing program, older boys who were Explorer Scouts completed the traditional Boy Scout advancement requirements to earn Eagle. Air Scouts in the 1940s wore Tenderfoot, Second Class, and First Class patches that featured two, three, or four blades on embroidered airplane propellers, then could work toward the Eagle Scout Award.

▲ QUARTERMASTER MEDAL

The medal for Quartermaster, Sea Scouting's highest rank, combines the emblem of the Boy Scouts of America with an anchor and a ship's wheel.

SCOUTING SKILLS AT SEA ▲ ▶

Following nautical tradition, Sea Scouts have always advanced from Apprentice to Ordinary and then Able before reaching Quartermaster, Sea Scouting's highest rank. Under the umbrella of the Venturing program, Sea Scouts can also earn the Venturing Silver Award. Those who attained the First Class rank before becoming Sea Scouts may continue advancing to Eagle.

THE PERSON BEHIND THE PIN ▶

Venturing's Silver Award, Sea Scouting's Quartermaster medal, and the Boy Scouts' Eagle Scout pin all symbolize high achievements of young people and their values, skills, and promise for the future.

Insignia and Emblems

A proud Eagle Scout standing in front
of the Capitol Building, Washington, D.C.

INSIGNIA AND EMBLEMS

"When Baden-Powell started the Scouting movement, he felt that any Scout who took the time and trouble to master skills should be rewarded for his effort. He gave to each Scout who passed certain tests a badge to wear on his uniform. It recognized the importance of what the Scout had done and let others know of his achievement."

1990 *Boy Scout Handbook*, p. 589

Evolution of the Eagle Scout Medal

At first, the highest rank of the Boy Scouts of America was to be the Silver Wolf, an award that Robert Baden-Powell had designated for outstanding British Scouts. Ernest Thompson Seton, one of the BSA's founders, had such a deep interest in wolves that he sometimes sketched a wolf footprint next to his signature. The 1910 "original" edition of the *Boy Scout Handbook*, borrowing heavily from the writings of both Seton and Baden-Powell, listed 14 badges of merit (none were ever produced) that First Class Scouts could earn. A boy who earned them all would be given the Silver Wolf (also never made). However, public opinion and the founders of the BSA felt a more fitting icon would be the symbol of the United States, an eagle.

The following year, the first truly American edition of the *Boy Scout Handbook* explained that First Class Scouts who earned 21 merit badges would be called Eagle Scouts, and would receive "an eagle's head in silver." The accompanying sketch of the proposed medal showed a different design, that of the profile of an eagle in flight. By the time Scouts began receiving their pins in 1912, the Eagle medal had changed again to the iconic form still recognized today.

1912–1915

▲ **T.H. FOLEY**
The New York City firm produced no more than 350 Eagle Awards, catalogued as THF 1. This one was presented to Arthur Eldred, the first Eagle Scout. The silver wash is gone, revealing the color of the bronze die-cast pendant.

1915–1930

▲ **DIEGES & CLUST / ROBBINS COMPANY**
When T.H. Foley went out of business, the BSA engaged Dieges & Clust to produce medals nearly identical to the THF 1. Five years later, the contract moved to the Robbins Company of Attleboro, Massachusetts, which made this, the ROB 1, from 1920–1930.

1930–1933

▲ **ROBBINS COMPANY**
Considered by many collectors to be the finest Eagle pendant ever made, the sterling silver ROB 2A had finely engraved details on the front and the back. Perhaps no more than 4,000 ROB 2As were made before being replaced with the slightly less distinct ROB 2B.

1933–1970

▲ **ROBBINS COMPANY**
The ROB 3 medal issued from 1933–1954 did not have the letters BSA across the pendant. It was followed in 1955 by the ROB 4 (shown here), featuring a smooth back suitable for engraving the name of the Eagle Scout receiving it and his court of honor date.

In 1915, details of the design and production of the original Eagle Scout Award were lost in a fire that burned down the T.H. Foley Company. Any papers that might have recorded the names of the artists responsible for crafting the first medal were destroyed. Since then, four other firms have been licensed by the BSA to manufacture the awards. To the delight of collectors, medals produced at different times exhibit slight variations. Even with its changes, though, the Eagle Scout medal is as recognizable today as it was when the first one was made a century ago.

| 1970–1978 | 1968–1999 | 1999–2007 | 2008–PRESENT |

▲ **ROBBINS COMPANY**
Significant changes highlighted the ROB 5, the last Eagle Award made by the Robbins Company. The full-feathered back returned (show above), replacing the smooth back of the ROB 4. The letters BSA, absent since 1933, appeared again across the front of the pendant.

▲ **STANGE COMPANY**
Added in 1968 as a second manufacturer of Eagle Scout Awards, the Stange Company continued to produce medals until 1999. This one, 1974's STG 3, matched the new logo of NESA, the National Eagle Scout Association.

▲ **CUSTOM FINE JEWELRY**
Custom Fine Jewelry of Fort Worth, Texas, began making Eagle Awards for the BSA in 1999. In the years that followed, the firm introduced laser design techniques that produced extremely sharp features to pendants including this CFJ 1.

▲ **STANGE COMPANY**
In 2008, the Stange Company was again chosen to produce medals for Eagle Scouts. The scroll features a cast knot introduced by Custom Fine Jewelry rather than one made of wire. Even so, the most recent medal looks remarkably like the first.

Making an Eagle Scout Medal

In its first hundred years, more than two million Scouts have earned the Eagle Scout Award, and more than two million medals have been made. Five different companies have produced the medals, each putting its own variations on the basic design. The manner of manufacturing the medals has changed, too, as have the materials incorporated in the finished work. Yet through all the alterations, the medal has maintained its recognizable appearance throughout the history of the Boy Scouts of America.

The first Eagle Scout medals were die struck. A reverse image of the medal was painstakingly carved into a die. A sheet of metal, in this case bronze, was placed between the two halves of the die and exposed to tremendous pressure, forcing the metal into the desired shape. The pendant and the scroll were washed with silver and assembled with a red, white, and blue ribbon.

Three years later the award's first manufacturer went out of business. Other firms stepped in and for the next 60 years Eagle Awards were made of sterling silver, an alloy of silver and a very small amount of another metal, such as copper, to give it strength.

The word sterling appeared on the backs of many Eagle scrolls and pendants of that era.

Steep increases in silver prices in 1980 caused the BSA to issue medals made of copper with a plating of silver. Sterling silver medals could be special-ordered from the National Council.

In 1993, pewter was added to the list of materials found in Eagle Scout Awards. Molten pewter was poured into centrifugal wheels that, when spun, forced the metal into molds. Today's awards are made with either sterling silver or non-sterling metals.

The third component of an Eagle Scout medal is the ribbon. It has changed in width, length, and the ways it attaches to the scroll but, like the pendant and scroll it unites, has remained essentially the same throughout the decades.

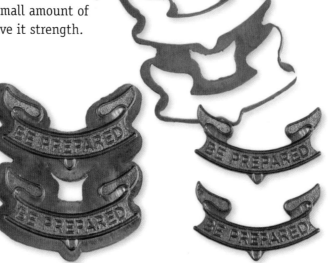

▲ ANCHORING IN
Posts fused to the back of the scroll serve as anchors for the pin assembly that a Scout will use to secure the medal to his uniform.

▲ STAMPING THE SCROLL
Pressure from a stamping machine forces the blank into a die that flattens the back and presses the Scout Motto, "Be Prepared," onto the front.

▲ TRIMMING
Excess metal is removed from around the scroll, and from the hole that will hold the wire knotted to represent the Scout slogan, "Do A Good Turn Daily."

▲ CUTTING IT TO SHAPE
One of several methods that have been used to make scrolls for Eagle Scout Awards begins by cutting a blank from a bar of copper.

SPINNING OUT PENDANTS ▶

Many Eagle pendants have been die cast in a manner similar to the creation of stamped scrolls. The pendants pictured here have been formed using centrifugal force to fill molds with molten metal. The molds have been broken away, revealing the pendants and surplus pewter.

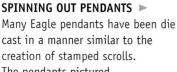

▲ FINISHING THE SCROLL

The shine and color of the scroll is the result of processes that can include oxidizing, silver plating, and lacquering. The last step is to add the hanging knot.

◀ FINAL TOUCHES

Like the scrolls, the final look of a pendant depends on treatments ranging from acid washing to silver plating.

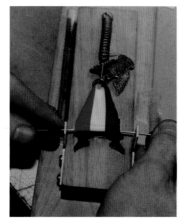

◀ PUTTING IT ALL TOGETHER

A craftsperson assembles the scroll, pendant, and ribbon to complete the Eagle Scout Award. This hands-on approach to finishing the medal has been done the same way for every Eagle pin made in the last hundred years.

▲ MEANING BEHIND THE MEDAL

Emerging from the heat and pressure of the manufacturing process, each of the two million Eagle Scout Awards that have been created honors an individual Scout who will make it his own and proudly carry it with him for the rest of his life.

Eagle Scout Palms

It was so unusual in Scouting's early years for a Scout to earn enough merit badges to receive the Eagle Scout Award that little thought was given to acknowledging anyone who might earn more. That had changed by the 1920s, bringing pressure on the Boy Scouts of America to create a rank above Eagle for those who completed significant numbers of additional merit badges. The answer came in the 1927 when the BSA's *Official Handbook for Boys* announced that Eagle Palms would be granted to indicate how many merit badges beyond 21 an Eagle Scout had earned. The Bronze Palm represented five additional merit badges. The Gold Palm stood for 10, and the Silver Palm indicated 15.

The numerical requirements for Eagle Palms are the same today. In addition, a Scout must be active in his troop and patrol for at least three months after becoming an Eagle, or after the awarding of the last Palm. He must demonstrate Scout spirit by living the Scout Oath and Law in his everyday life, and make a satisfactory effort to develop and demonstrate leadership ability. As with the ranks of Tenderfoot through Eagle, a Scout completing the requirements for Palm appears before a board of review. Palms can be worn on the ribbon of the Eagle Award or pinned to the embroidered Eagle Scout knot.

The BSA does not document Scouts who have earned every merit badge, but estimates put the number at fewer than 200. The first mention of that feat in *Boys' Life* magazine was a 1979 article featuring Robert E. Cahill, Jr., of Levittown, Pennsylvania. "I never planned on getting all of the merit badges," he told the magazine. "I just kept getting them." The last of his 125 merit badges was American Cultures. And then he was done.

▲ BRONZE EAGLE PALM
Granted to an Eagle Scout for earning five additional merit badges.

▲ GOLD EAGLE PALM
Granted for earning 10 additional merit badges.

▲ SILVER EAGLE PALM
Granted for earning 15 additional merit badges.

CHARTING THE POSSIBILITIES ▷
Eagle Scouts who earn more than the 15 merit badges indicated by a Silver Eagle Palm can wear combinations of Palms. This chart shows the correct combinations and their required tenure in 2012.

Palm numbers	Merit badges beyond those required for Eagle Scout	Total merit badges since joining Scouts	Minimum number of months since earning Eagle	Number of Palms to be worn		
				Bronze	Gold	Silver
1	5	26	3	1		
2	10	31	6		1	
3	15	36	9			1
4	20	41	12	1		1
5	25	46	15		1	1
6	30	51	18			2
7	35	56	21	1		2
8	40	61	24		1	2
9	45	66	27			3
10	50	71	30	1		3
11	55	76	33		1	3
12	60	81	36			4
13	65	86	39	1		4
14	70	91	42		1	4
15	75	96	45			5
16	80	101	48	1		5
17	85	106	51		1	5
18	90	111	54			6
19	95	116	57	1		6
20	100	121	60		1	6

EARNING THEM ALL ▶
Clay Wood of Troop 5048, Jackson, Ohio, is one of the few Eagle Scouts to have earned every merit badge. His total of 128 includes two historic badges that could be earned only during the BSA's Centennial year. He found that the easiest merit badge to complete was Collections, and that Scuba Diving was the most difficult. He also faced the challenge of figuring out how to display all of his awards, including the row of Eagle Palms across the top of his sash.

Eagle Scouting's Medal Man

"Put your arms out and embrace all these young men that get their Eagle Award, because all of them—for generations—have done it and done it well."

REVEREND DR. TERRY GROVE, ON RECEIVING THE DISTINGUISHED EAGLE SCOUT AWARD

Thirty years ago, at his son's Eagle court of honor, the Reverend Dr. Terry Grove had a sudden realization. "I noticed that the Eagle Scout Award medal that I received as a boy in 1956 was different from the one that my son had just received," he recalls. "Mine was clearly sterling silver. The letters 'BSA' were not on the chest of the Eagle pendant and the pendant's back was flat. On the other hand, my son's Eagle pendant was not sterling, had a BSA on the chest, and feathers engraved on the back." There were other Eagle Scouts attending the court of honor who represented a range of generations. Each of their pins was distinct, too.

The discovery piqued Dr. Grove's curiosity. Why did the details differ from one Eagle Scout pin to another? What did that say about the award itself?

Soon he was reading all he could find in collectors' magazines about Eagle Scout Awards, and he sought out those who had collections of Eagle memorabilia. He learned about manufacturers, production years, markings, and differences in production methods. At a 1988 National Order of the Arrow Conference, he joined 11 Scouters with medal collections for a long night of discussing the badges. That led to a cooperative effort to develop a comprehensive listing of the evolution of the Eagle Scout Awards, and Dr. Grove was encouraged to build a collection of his own. Today it has grown into the largest and most important collection of Eagle Scout medals in the world.

"When I started doing this in the 1980s and 1990s there weren't that many other people collecting Eagle medals," he explains. "I was able to trade for some and bought others." In 1991 he published *The Comprehensive Guide to the Eagle Scout Award*, an exhaustive study of the medals, patches, and hat pins that Eagle Scouts could wear on their uniforms. "To gather data for the book, I interviewed nearly 300 people," he says. "Many of them donated their medals to the collection."

Rather than keep the medals to himself, Dr. Grove developed displays that tell the story of Scouting's highest rank through its historic artifacts. The displays span the history of the Eagle Scout Award from its beginnings to the present day, providing a comprehensive look at the heritage of Scouting's recognition for those who have reached its highest rank. "I love to do the research and find the stories of what was going on," he explains, "but the real joy is in sharing with others."

◄ PRIZED POSSESSION

Among the thousands of pins, patches, and papers in his collection, Terry Grove's most cherished item is his own Eagle Scout Award. It represents all he achieved and all he gained as a Boy Scout.

▲ **EAGLE OF DISTINCTION**

For exemplary service to his community, his profession, and to Scouting, Dr. Grove was declared a Distinguished Eagle Scout in 2011 by the BSA's National Council. "It doesn't matter when we got the Eagle Scout Award," he said in his acceptance remarks. "What it means is we prepared ourselves well for the world that we live in."

▲▼ **ENDURING LEGACY**

Terry Grove's displays of Eagle Scout memorabilia have been exhibited at the National Scouting Museum in Irving, Texas, and at national jamborees and Order of the Arrow Conferences. Thousands of people have enjoyed tracing the development of the emblems through the years. According to Dr. Grove, "The fun thing is to watch a father bring his son in and walk over and say, 'That's my Eagle. That's what mine looked like.'"

Eagle Scout Service

Eagle Service Project
(1978) by Joseph Csatari.

EAGLE SCOUT SERVICE
"There is a major difference between the service project for Star and Life, and that for Eagle. In the first two you can be a follower. For Eagle you must be a leader. You must plan, develop, and give leadership to a project of help to any religious group, school, or community. The project must be of real value when finished."

1979 *Boy Scout Handbook*, p. 463

Building Eagle Scout Trails, 1924–1934

"Enclosed you will please find a draft of a proposal whereby boys who have attained the rank of Eagle Scout shall be permitted to give of themselves and their services toward the development of our nation-wide playground system." Thus began a 1923 letter from Edgar G. Maclay, president of the North Central Montana Council of the Boy Scouts of America, to Stephen Mather, superintendent of the National Park Service.

In each park, Mr. Maclay explained, "Eagle Scouts...shall map out, construct, post and dedicate a new Trail leading from some well known point to a certain definite objective. These Trails in each case to be forever known as Eagle Scout Trail."

Superintendent Mather responded favorably to the idea, and in the summer of 1924, 32 Eagle Scouts from around the Northwest set up camp in the backcountry of Yellowstone National Park and built five miles of hiking trail. The following year, the program expanded to Glacier National Park in Montana and Mt. Rainier in Washington. Thereafter, it was continued only in Glacier until 1934.

"This is the best trail in the park," said Yellowstone Superintendent Horace Albright upon the completion of the first Eagle Scout Trail. "You boys who have come here this summer are trail-blazers in a double sense; you have made this physical trail and you have established a precedent which will be followed with the benefit to all."

◄▲ WORKING THE ROUTE

Eagle Scouts used axes, picks, two-man saws, and shovels to clear trees and brush along new locations, then shaped the tread for hiking trails. Work on the Eagle Scout Trails set high standards that continue today as Scouts engage in environmental Good Turns for public lands and in BSA camps across the nation.

◄ SIGN OF SUCCESS

Pathways constructed by Eagle Scouts were significant by the standards of the day. The first Yellowstone crew reported the completion of five miles of trail. In the more rugged terrain of Glacier National Park, Scouts built between 2,500 feet and 4,700 feet of new tread each summer. Rustic signs at trailheads credited Eagle Scouts for their efforts.

◄ HIGH ADVENTURE

Eagle Scouts in full uniform pose at the end of their work on an Eagle Scout Trail. They had lived in backcountry camps, cooked over open fires, slept in tents, and come away with plenty of stories to share with family and friends back home.

HIGH COUNTRY ACCESS ▼ ►

The Eagle Scout Trail built along the shoreline of St. Mary's Lake led hikers close to steep mountains of Glacier National Park. An embroidered patch, available to Scouts involved with the construction, featured a mountain goat—Glacier's iconic emblem.

THE TRAIL'S TRUE DESTINATION ►

"The strong point that I am endeavoring to develop is the spirit of service amongst boys," Edgar Maclay wrote as the primary reason for encouraging Eagle Scouts to roll up their sleeves and do a significant good turn for the land. "I believe that the amount of service that they can be inspired to render will be a measure of the fullness of their citizenship."

Three Eagle Scout Projects in Guatemala

A trip to Guatemala with his father Mark to learn Spanish led 13-year-old Will Troppe to an Eagle Scout project that would change lives in Central America and in his hometown of Alexandria, Virginia. While taking classes at the Centro Linguistico La Unión, Will realized that the town of Vuelta Grande badly needed a water treatment system and help repairing and expanding its school.

Back in America, Will convinced fellow Troop 167 Scouts Chris Stephens and Tom Mosher to join him in directing their Eagle projects toward Vuelta Grande. Will spent much of the next two years organizing the return trip to Guatemala.

When he finally got there, Will brought with him Scouts, leaders, and family members, 28 in all. The group visited in local homes, explored the surrounding landscape, and helped complete three Eagle projects: Chris Stephens' chlorine-based water filtration system, Tom Mosher's improvements to the village school, and Will's solutions for serious erosion problems.

▲ **CEMENTING THE FUTURE**

"We didn't want to do a one-shot thing," Mark Troppe told *Eagletter*, the magazine of the National Eagle Scout Association. "We really wanted to do something that was part of an ongoing project. We hoped, and we continue to hope, that there would be other Scouts from around the United States who might be interested in doing something like this."

WORTH THE EFFORT ▶

The group shared in the lives of Vuelta Grande families as they worked together to complete the Eagle Scout projects. The improvements in the village will have a positive and lasting impact, and the friendships and new understanding between Guatemalans and Americans will endure.

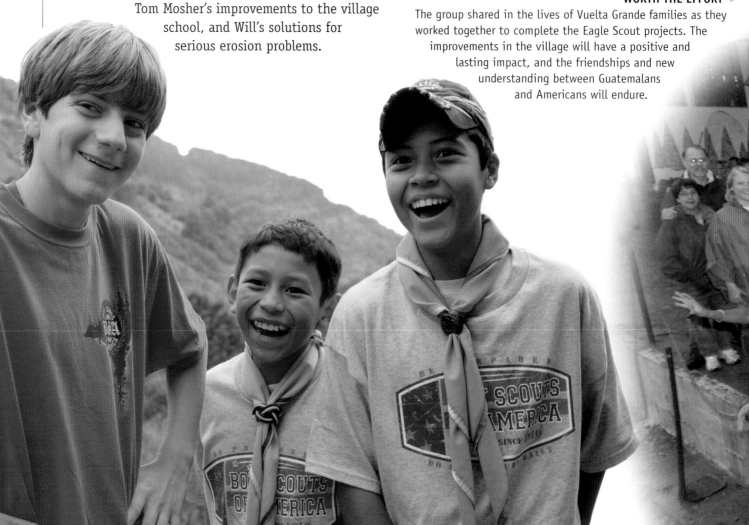

▲ GETTING IT DONE

Language barriers and cultural differences fell by the wayside as boys from Alexandria, Virginia, and Vuelta Grande, Guatemala discovered common ground working on projects designed to protect the environment and enhance opportunities for learning.

▲ A VISION IN ACTION

"One of the things that we tried to do is demonstrate the value of working together and the things that it can accomplish," Mark Troppe reported. Troop 167's trio of Guatemalan Eagle Scout projects certainly accomplished that, and much, much more.

Project Russian Playground

Sometimes giving back means going back. For Alex Griffith, the journey was long both in miles and in years.

Born in Krasnoyarsk, Russia, the third largest city in Siberia, Alex spent the first year of his life in Children's Hospital No. 20, an orphanage for abandoned children. Undernourished and ill, he was adopted by Dwight and Jenny Griffith, who brought him to his new home in Jarrettsville, Maryland.

Alex grew up as a typical American boy and a Scout earning his way through the ranks. Thinking about a worthwhile Eagle Scout project, his mind turned to the place where he had been an infant. His parents had a photograph of the Siberian orphanage where 400 children still lived, and he noticed that the playground was just a sand pit with one crooked swing.

Though it was half a world away, Alex decided to build a real playground for the children to enjoy. Finding people to assist him led to Tatiana Khegay, president of the Krasnoyarsk-Yenisei Rotary Club, who helped smooth the way in Russia. Rotary clubs in America also came to his aid, and his fellow Scouts in Troop 809 pitched in to help raise the $62,000 he needed.

Alex designed the equipment for the playground, which the manufacturer agreed to construct at a discount and package for shipment. Alex traveled to Siberia with three other Scouts and two adult leaders. Soon the new playground was in place and the laughter of children rang out through the Russian day.

"Not only has he affected the lives of us, living in Jarrettsville, but he has also affected the lives of so many around the world with his Eagle project," said Troop 809 Scoutmaster Dave Kraft. "Alex has proven himself a true representative of the values instilled by the Boy Scouts of America and has passed those qualities on to others around the world."

◄ **WHERE IT ALL BEGAN**
Alex Griffith's Eagle Scout project led him to help others and to discover much about himself as he visited the orphanage in Siberia where he had lived as a baby.

▲ **SHOULDER TO SHOULDER**
Russian and American volunteers united to smooth the sand pit next to the orphanage, assemble the playground equipment, and put it in place.

CARVING OUT A HERITAGE ►
A chainsaw artist created an American eagle and a Russian bear to stand at the playground entrance as emblems of international friendship.

▲ CELEBRATING SUCCESS

On his 16th birthday, Alex Griffith took part in the opening ceremony of the new playground in Krasnoyarsk. In recognition of his Eagle Scout project, which had taken hundreds of hours and involved volunteers on two continents, Alex received the inaugural Glenn A. and Melinda W. Adams National Eagle Scout Service Project of the Year Award.

Eagles Saving Lives

In 1911, the year before the first Eagle Scout pin was awarded, more than two dozen boys were given the Honor Medal for saving lives. "It not only signifies that the Scout has saved life at the risk of his own," the National Council explained, "but it also recognizes the training that the Scout has undergone to make him ready for such an emergency." The Honor Medals were granted as bronze, silver, or gold, depending on the risk incurred by the Scout.

The two awards soon become entwined as many Eagles acted on their Scouting experience and values to rescue people in danger. In fact, the same month that he learned he was to be the BSA's first Eagle, Arthur Eldred saved a fellow Scout from drowning and became one of the early winners of a bronze Honor Medal.

Through the decades, citations for BSA Honor Medals have noted a variety of heroic deeds—from the rescue of a man who had fallen through thin ice to a Scout on a sinking ship sending calls for help over a wireless telegraph. Many of the awards have involved saving someone from drowning.

Scouts responded in nearly every case with cool heads even in difficult circumstances. Eagle Scout Lyman Boyle was in a leaky boat with several men and two young girls. In deep water near a dam, the boat capsized. "The girls could not swim," Boyle reported. "All the men swam to shore and I was left alone with the girls. They grabbed on to each other. I parted the girls and put one of them on the upturned side of the boat, and as the other girl was going down for the third time I grabbed her and towed her in with the cross chest carry a few yards from land, where I was given help."

Close to 6,000 Honor Medals and Heroism Awards have been granted in Scouting's history, many to Eagle Scouts and to boys who would go on to earn the Eagle Scout Award.

▲ HEROISM AWARD
Given to youth and adult BSA members, the Heroism Award recognizes lifesaving acts involving minimum risk to one's own safety.

▲ HONOR MEDAL
The Honor Medal is awarded to a Scout or Scouter who has demonstrated unusual heroism and skill in saving or attempting to save life at considerable risk to self. Extreme risk adds crossed palms to the award.

▲ TREVOR ROBINSON
Walking with classmate Krista Benson, Eagle Scout Trevor Robinson of Gold River, California, suddenly saw a car speeding right at them. He disregarded his own safety to push Krista out of harm's way. The automobile hit him as he tried to jump clear, breaking his collarbone. For his heroic action, Trevor was given the Honor Medal with crossed palms by the Boy Scouts of America, and the deep gratitude of Krista, her family, and friends.

▲ MARSHALL OLIPHANT

The December, 1928, issue of *Boys' Life* magazine reported that "During a picnic on the shores of Lake Erie, Mr. Phillip Kennedy swam out some distance and was taken with a cramp. Scout Oliphant swam out to him, and after a struggle brought Mr. Kennedy, who weighed fifty more pounds than the Scout did, ashore." Oliphant lived in Cleveland Heights, Ohio.

▲ LYMAN BOYLE

The Eagle Scout from Troop 4, Frankfort, Indiana, earned the gold Honor Medal for his 1926 rescue of two girls in danger of drowning. The First Class patrol leader patch on his sleeve showed he also served as a leader in his troop.

A TRUE STORY ▶

Scouts in Action is a monthly feature of *Boys' Life* magazine. Through the decades it has provided colorful accounts of Scouts, including Eagle Arthur Joseph Scott, who were given Honor Medals or Heroism Awards for saving lives.

Presidential Encounters

"I heartily wish all good luck to the movement." The final words of the 1911 *Boy Scout Handbook* were written by former United States president Theodore Roosevelt. A strong supporter of the Boy Scouts of America, Roosevelt saw the organization as a positive force, and he became the BSA's first honorary vice-president and only Chief Scout Citizen.

Every subsequent president has lent support by serving as the BSA's honorary president while in office. Some have been Scouts or adult leaders, and many have spoken at national jamborees. Gerald Ford advanced to Scouting's highest rank.

"One of the proudest moments of my life came in the court of honor when I was awarded the Eagle Scout badge. I still have that badge," President Ford told the Boy Scouts. "It is a treasured possession." He added that three great principles of Scouting—self-discipline, teamwork, and moral and patriotic values—are the basic building blocks of leadership. "I applaud the Scouting program for continuing to emphasize them."

FRANKLIN D. ROOSEVELT ▶

Through economic depression and world war, President Roosevelt relied on Scouts to serve their communities and the nation.

▲ **WILLIAM HOWARD TAFT**
President Taft became the BSA's first honorary president in 1910, saying, "I am very glad to give my sympathy and support to such a movement as this. Anything that directs the boy's spirit in the right channel for usefulness and for the making of manly men should be encouraged."

▲ **HARRY S. TRUMAN**
"What a greater nation this would be if the principles of Scouting could be woven more closely into our daily lives." President Truman.

◀ **PRESIDENTIAL WELCOMES**
Presidents of the United States have been welcoming Eagle Scouts to the White House for more than a century. Under the terms of its 1916 Congressional charter, the BSA reports yearly to the speaker of the House of Representatives. The Report to the Nation contingent also visits the president, briefing him on the state of Scouting and receiving encouragement to continue striving toward the BSA's goals.

John F. Kennedy

Ronald Reagan

George W. Bush

Barack Obama

When you help start a Scout troop, there's no guarantee one of the Scouts will grow up to be President.

But you never know.

For all the facts on how your organization can support a Scout troop, call Boy Scouts of America. The Trinity Methodist Church of Grand Rapids, Michigan did, and look what they've got to show for it.

SCOUTING USA

Prepared as a Public Service by Foote, Cone & Belding, Inc.

Flights of
Eagles

The launch of Apollo 11, commanded
by Eagle Scout Neil Armstrong.

Eagle Scout Family

"Program, program, program!" That's how Scoutmaster Carl Imhoff sums up the success of Troop 190 in Richland, Washington. By encouraging plenty of adventures planned and carried out by the boys, the troop has kept older Scouts so involved that more than 30 have earned the Eagle Scout Award. Carl has enjoyed the added satisfaction of sharing Scouting with his sons, all of them Eagles.

"I tell Carl that I may not be much of an adventurer," his wife Kristen says, "but I gave him three sons who would go hiking with him whenever he wanted."

"Kristen has been very supportive," Carl adds. "Being a Scoutmaster means doing something every day, and that requires lots of teamwork at home."

Both recognize the power of Scouting to reinforce family values. "I care about character and integrity, and Scouting plays into that," Kristen says. She speaks highly of the BSA's emphasis on leadership and service to the community. "That's where Scouting really excels. I saw leadership being taught and practiced at patrol leader meetings around our kitchen table. It helped us bring those ideals to our kids."

Troop 190 schedules a high adventure trek every year, plus a 50-mile backpacking trip. With the Cascade Mountains nearby for rafting, hiking, and skiing, Richland Scouts can reach the backcountry for weekend adventures, too.

"Being a Scouting family means there are going to be lots of times when they are gone, and lots of laundry when they come back home," Kristen laughs. "Even so, I knew I was really committed when I bought a cookie cutter in the shape of an Eagle Scout Award to make cookies for all the courts of honor."

◀ ▼ FAMILY LEGACY

A Scout in Troop 77, Fayetteville, Arkansas, Carl Imhoff went to the Westark Area Council's Camp Orr on the Buffalo River, first as a camper and then as a summer staff first aid instructor. "We worked on our Scout skills, swam in the river, and pulled off ticks," he remembers. "It was great!" A generation later, he and his wife Kristen celebrated the Scouting achievements of their sons (from left) Daniel, Kurt, and Bob.

Imhoff Named Eagle Scout

CARL IMHOFF

Carl Imhoff was awarded th[e] Eagle Badge of Scouting, at

◄ CLIMBING TOGETHER

"My favorite part of Scouting is the outdoor stuff," Bob Imhoff says. "That was a way for me to go out and do things with my brothers and my dad. Our family has shared that together." Ascending 12,281-foot Mt. Adams in the Washington Cascades was his first trip on a big mountain. "We camped halfway up, and there was a howling wind all night. But by morning the wind had died and we climbed steep snow toward the summit. We made it to the top, then glissaded all the way back down."

▼ MAKING THEIR MARK

In the role of a logger with the long-ago Continental Tie and Lumber Company, Daniel Imhoff demonstrated pole climbing during one of his summers on the staff at Philmont, the BSA's high adventure base in northern New Mexico. His father, Carl, had been a ranger at Philmont during his own college summers, leading Scouts as they set off for 10-day backpacking treks. Kurt Imhoff has been a ranger, too, and Bob has his application in.

FOLLOW ME, BOYS! ▲

Kurt Imhoff (standing at left during a journey in the Goat Rocks Wilderness, 150 miles south of Seattle) has always been fascinated by maps and trail guidebooks. During his years with Troop 190, he became a driving force in suggesting routes, figuring out logistics, and taking on leadership roles of increasing responsibility.

Eagle Scouts in Space

Leadership, bravery, determination, and a spirit of adventure—these Eagle Scout qualities characterize many who have strapped themselves into the planet's fastest vehicles and blasted free of the Earth's gravity. Of the more than 300 pilots and scientists who have flown on NASA missions, two-thirds have had Scouting experience, and of these, over three dozen held the rank of Eagle Scout.

Scouts today who are following the Trail to Eagle will almost certainly become some of America's space explorers of the future. Many are involved with the BSA's STEM initiative, a program which emphasizes *science*, *technology*, *engineering*, and *mathematics*.

With this and all the other opportunities provided by Scouting, those who become Eagle Scouts are well prepared to pursue any profession that fires their imaginations, even one that may someday send them to the Moon and beyond.

SCOUTING THE MOON ▲ ▶
On July 20, 1969, Neil Armstrong became the first person to walk on the Moon. Eagle Scout Armstrong had gained much of his early training with his Scout troop (that's him in the back row, far right). Three years later, Charles Duke was the second Eagle to step on to the lunar surface. All but one of the twelve astronauts who have stood on the Moon were Scouts.

▼ **ULTIMATE SACRIFICE**
Three Eagle Scouts have been killed during NASA missions. Ellison Onizuka (pictured far left) perished with the rest of his crew when the space shuttle Challenger exploded after take-off in 1986. Roger Chaffee lost his life during a launch test for Apollo 1, and William McCool died when the shuttle Columbia broke up on re-entry into the Earth's atmosphere.

E.O. Wilson

Among the world's most influential and honored scientists, Edward O. Wilson found the subjects that would be his life's work while he was a Scout. "The Boy Scouts of America seemed invented just for me," he wrote in *Naturalist*, his best-selling autobiography. "The 1940 *Handbook for Boys*, which I purchased for half a dollar, became my most cherished possession."

That edition of the *Handbook* was filled with information about outdoor life, but what truly caught his attention were the sections on zoology and botany with "page after page of animals and plants wonderfully well illustrated, explaining where to find them, how to identify them." Wilson went on to explain how, "The public schools and church had offered nothing like this. The Boy Scouts legitimated Nature as the center of my life."

He earned 46 merit badges in all, recalling that "I happily crunched through the programs for subjects as diverse as Bird Study, Farm Records and Book-Keeping, Life Saving, Journalism, and Public Health."

He received his PhD in biology from Harvard University in 1955. Field research in many parts of the world established him as an expert in the study of ants. He expanded on what he learned from them to develop important theories of biodiversity and sociobiology, encompassing many species, in an effort to understand the underpinnings of entire societies.

Well into his 80s, Dr. Wilson continues to write and teach at Harvard as Pellegrino University Research Professor in Entomology for the Department of Organismic and Evolutionary Biology.

EAGLE SCOUT INSECT COLLECTOR ▲

"I never met a bully in the Scouts, and relatively few braggarts," E.O. Wilson has said of his years in Scouting. "The questions before each boy were: Can you walk twenty miles, tie a tourniquet, save a swimmer in Red Cross lifeguard exercises, build a sturdy sapling bridge with nothing but axe and rope? For me the answers were yes, yes, yes!"

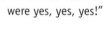
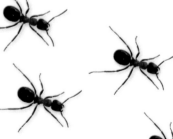

INSECT LIFE

MERIT BADGE SERIES

BOY SCOUTS OF AMERIC[A]

An Ant dairymaid and her cows. The Ant protects the Aphids from enemies, and in return obtains honeydew. Ants will stroke the Aphids with their feelers, to induce them to give off extra drops.

◄ **INSECT LIFE MERIT BADGE**

When he opened the *Insect Life* merit badge pamphlet for the first time, E.O. Wilson's heart sang. The requirements asked him to show an examiner the natural surroundings in which certain insects lived, find living specimens of the insects, and tell of their habits or of the nature of their fitness for their particular surroundings. It was a merit badge that would change his life.

▲ A MAN AND HIS ANT
"Most children have a bug period," E.O. Wilson remarked in *Naturalist*, "I never grew out of mine." Dr. Wilson has written two dozen books, receiving Pulitzer Prizes for *On Human Nature* and as co-author (with Bert Hölldobler) of *The Ants*. Among many other honors, he was named one of *Time* magazine's 25 Most Influential Americans of 1995.

Eagle Scout Athletes

A Scout reciting the Oath promises "to keep myself physically strong." For many Eagle Scouts, that translates into participating in sports, from friendly neighborhood games to playing in leagues and on high school teams.

Eagle Scouts also count among their ranks a number of collegiate and professional athletes. Future U.S. President Gerald Ford was voted most valuable player on the 1934 University of Michigan football team.

Distinguished Eagle Scout Jim Mora played football for Occidental College and coached the New Orleans Saints and Indianapolis Colts. As starting wide receiver for the Chicago Bears, Emery Moorehead helped the team win the 1985 Super Bowl. Chan Gailey coached college teams and has been head coach of the Dallas Cowboys and Buffalo Bills. On the basketball court, 7-foot center John Koncak starred with the Atlanta Hawks. Bill Bradley is in the Basketball Hall of Fame.

WILLIE BANKS ▶

Upbeat and enthused by competition, Eagle Scout Willie Banks represented the United States in three Olympic Games and won a silver medal at the 1983 World Championships. He set a world record of almost 59 feet for the triple jump—a hop, skip, and jump into a sand pit. As a student athlete, he completed an undergraduate degree at the University of California, Los Angeles, then attended the UCLA School of Law. In 1999 Willie Banks was inducted into the National Track and Field Hall of Fame.

◀ **JEREMY GUTHRIE**

Eagle Scout Jeremy Guthrie pitched the Stanford Cardinal to the College World Series. He was called up to the major league in 2006 by the Cleveland Indians, then played five seasons for the Baltimore Orioles before moving on to the Colorado Rockies. Other Eagle Scout baseball players include five-time All-Star Albert Belle (Indians, White Sox, and Orioles) and Shane Victorino, right fielder for the 2008 World Series champion Philadelphia Phillies.

Public Servant Eagles

The leadership skills developed by Eagle Scouts have guided many into careers of public service at local, state, and national levels. As teachers, fire fighters, police officers, and members of the military, they draw on their Scouting backgrounds to make good things happen. Eagles who seek elected office bring to the ballot the values they have carried with them since they first recited the Scout Oath and Law.

Fifteen current state governors were Scouts, and four earned the Eagle award. More than 20 United States senators have been Eagles, and dozens of members of the House of Representatives. President Gerald R. Ford, who had been a Republican congressman from Michigan, was an Eagle Scout, too.

The national election of 1998 saw the Democratic ticket headed by two Eagle Scouts—Massachusetts Governor Michael Dukakis running for president and Senator Lloyd Bentsen of Texas vying to become vice-president. Senator Bill Bradley threw his hat into the presidential ring in 2000, as did Jon Huntsman (the former governor of Utah) in 2012. Both are Eagle Scouts.

Tom C. Clark earned his Eagle badge in 1914, an award he still prized when named a Supreme Court Justice in 1949. Current Justice Stephen Breyer is Eagle Scouting's other representative on the high court.

NEW YORK MAYOR MICHAEL BLOOMBERG ▼
"Being an Eagle Scout means that you took control of your own life," Mayor Bloomberg explained to Alvin Townley in the book *Legacy of Honor*. "You set an objective, a reasonably complex one for a young man, and that you pursued it through difficult times. Not every merit badge is easy. Sometimes things don't work out and you fail. But the person you see in the mirror is the person who should be most proud that you became an Eagle."

AMBASSADOR GARY LOCKE ▲ ▶
The first American of Chinese descent to serve as a governor, Gary Locke of Washington State was named Commerce Secretary by President Barack Obama, then succeeded Jon Huntsman (another Eagle Scout) as U.S. Ambassador to China. "You say that you're an Eagle, and automatically people expect more from you," Locke told Alvin Townley, "and that will continue throughout your life. Eagles are special. They've already shown perseverance, they've shown leadership qualities, and they've shown the ability to get things done, to accomplish things."

Eagles Who Mean Business

Stephen Bechtel, Jr. attributes much of his success to the Boy Scouts of America. "The best thing about the experience was what I learned in the way of character," he says. "Moral ethics, work ethics, decisiveness." With that foundation of values, he helped expand the Bechtel firm into a corporation operating on a global scale.

Like many business leaders who reached the Eagle rank, Mr. Bechtel has supported Scouting, too. The Bechtel Family Foundation's $50 million grant made possible the development of the newest BSA high adventure base, the Summit Bechtel Reserve, in the mountains of West Virginia.

"I wanted to give back to the Boy Scouts because of what they did for me, and more importantly for what they do for the young men of the country," he says. "Eagle Scouts are the next generation of leadership for the country."

Among the many other Eagles who mean business are Sam Walton (founder of Walmart), Alan Ashton (co-founder of WordPerfect), and CEOs John W. Creighton, Jr. (Weyerhaeuser), Gary Rogers (Dreyer's Ice Cream), Jim Rogers (Kampgrounds of America), Walter Scott, Jr. (Peter Kiewit Sons), Walter Wriston (Citicorp) and Rex Tillerson (ExxonMobil).

J.W. MARRIOTT, JR. ▶

"Many years ago, I joined Boy Scout Troop 241 in Chevy Chase, Maryland," J.W. "Bill" Marriott recalls. "It was one of the most rewarding and difficult experiences of my life. Finally, I achieved the highest Boy Scout honor, that of becoming an Eagle Scout. It took a lot of hard work and determination." As the CEO of Marriott International, one of the world's largest lodging companies, Mr. Marriott is always excited "to have former Scouts come work for Marriott because I know the lessons they've learned from Scouting, such as leadership and teamwork, will make them great employees for our company."

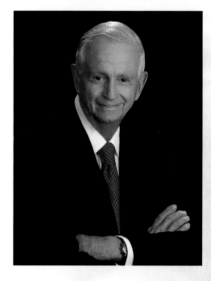

◀ **CHARLES PIGOTT**

Chairman of PACCAR, a builder of trucks and heavy equipment, Charles Pigott volunteered in 1986 to serve as president of the BSA's National Council. His son, Tom Pigott, is also an Eagle, and has been president of the Chief Seattle Council. "What I truly appreciate now," Tom says, "and why I'm involved with the Scouts as an adult is because the lessons and values that are taught to boys are invaluable in creating adult leaders for today."

◀ ▼ **SCOTT OKI**

As senior vice president for sales and marketing, Scott Oki was the driving force behind Microsoft's expansion into international markets. After ten years of 100-hour work weeks, though, it was time for a change.

Mr. Oki left Microsoft to spend time with his family, help his sons follow in his footsteps by becoming Eagle Scouts, and focus on community service that is increasing inner-city youth participation in Scouting. Still pushing big visions, he says, "If ninety percent of boys become Eagle Scouts, we could transform society."

Art of the Eagle: 1

A Tenderfoot whittles a neckerchief slide in the shape of an eagle and dreams of things to come. A world-famous artist applies brush to canvas and illustrates Eagle Scouts in action. Throughout the history of the Boy Scouts of America, many have sought to capture the spirit of the Eagle in works of art. For materials, they have turned to bronze and silver, paper and pen, or a sharp pocketknife and a good piece of pine. Embroidered patches have transformed colored thread into tightly stitched Eagle Scout emblems. Souvenirs ranging from clocks and key chains to holographic crystal cubes have highlighted many courts of honor celebrating the achievement of Scouting's highest rank. Whether the finished product is a painting worthy of hanging in a museum or an oddly-carved Eagle slide holding a Tenderfoot's neckerchief in place, art celebrating the BSA's highest rank inspires those who create it, those who appreciate it, and especially those who understand that the ideals of the BSA are infused throughout every effort to represent the art of the eagle.

EVER ONWARD ▶

Used for the 50th anniversary cover of *Boys' Life* magazine, Norman Rockwell's *Ever Onward* painting placed an Eagle at the center of Scouting. Mr. Rockwell joined the staff of *Boys' Life* magazine in 1912 at the age of 18, too old to become an Eagle Scout himself. For the next six decades he produced hundreds of paintings and illustrations of BSA scenes, many featuring Eagle Scouts. They appeared on calendars, in magazines, and as covers of Boy Scout handbooks and issues of *Boys' Life*.

A FITTING SUBJECT ▶

An eagle is an inviting subject for artists to portray. As a symbol of America, it is already rich with meaning. The strength and high-soaring characteristics of eagles in the wild lend obvious parallels to the qualities of Eagle Scouts. Graceful in flight, an eagle comes across as serious, noble, and focused in purpose and resolve.

CHARACTER COUNTS

Artwork through the decades has promoted the values of the Boy Scouts of America. This wall poster, released in 1961, features an Eagle Scout and "Strengthen America... Character Counts," the slogan of the BSA's 51st anniversary.

Art of the Eagle: 3

EAGLE SCOUT PLAZA ▶

Near the entrance to the Dallas, Texas, offices of the Circle Ten Council, a large bronze eagle touches down in the center of Eagle Scout Plaza. Circle Ten Scouts who become Eagles are honored by having their names engraved in granite paving stones surrounding the statue.

◀ **MEANINGFUL MESSAGES**

Printed programs for Eagle courts of honor often associate Scouts who have earned the BSA's highest rank with strong images of the American bald eagle. An eagle also highlights this brochure that encourages Eagle Scouts of all ages to enhance their involvement with the BSA through the National Eagle Scout Association.

There is no end
to the Eagle Scout trail.

If you are an Eagle Scout, join the National Eagle Scout Association.

www.nesa.org

◄ TRAIL TO MANHOOD

The Eagle Scout statue greeting troops at Philmont Scout Ranch is the bronze creation of sculptor Peter Fillerup. Seven feet tall and weighing over 800 pounds, the statue represents an ideal Eagle Scout from Troop 78, Fillerup's troop in Cody, Wyoming. Installed at Philmont's camping headquarters in 1984, it has watched over thousands of Scouts setting off on backcountry adventures.

▼ NATIONAL SCOUTING MUSEUM

A twin of Peter Fillerup's *Trail to Manhood* statue strides across the lawn of the National Scouting Museum in Irving, Texas. Open to all Scouts and the general public, the museum houses hundreds of thousands of patches, uniforms, and other treasures from Scouting's first hundred years. The museum is also home to the BSA collection of Norman Rockwell's Scouting paintings.

Eagle Scout Memorial Fountain

Built in 1910, New York City's Pennsylvania Station was a landmark of classic architecture and soaring grandeur. It covered seven acres in midtown Manhattan and served both as the terminal for the Pennsylvania Railroad and a spectacular entry point for travelers coming into the city. Above the columns of each of the station's main entrances stood a large clock encircled by a marble wreath and topped by an hour glass. Leaning against the sides of the clock were statues of two maidens, each with an eagle standing at her feet.

When the demolition of Penn Station began in 1963, John E. Starr, a past president of the Kansas City Area Council, suggested that one of the clock sculptures be moved to Kansas City, Missouri, to become a monument honoring Eagle Scouts. The board of the Pennsylvania Railroad agreed, and the sculpture was shipped by flat car to the Midwest. The Kansas City Parks and Recreation Department provided a location in the city's Hyde Park. Local firms designed and constructed the concrete fountain and landscaping, before the sculpture was installed. In place of the clock, the centerpiece became an Eagle Scout Award made of aluminum.

Eagle Scout Memorial Fountain was dedicated in the autumn of 1968. A book placed in the cornerstone contained the names of 14,000 Kansas City area Eagle Scouts who had earned the award.

THE ARTIST

Sculpted by Adolph A. Weinman in 1906, the maidens represent *Day* (left) and *Night*. Weinman gained further fame a decade later with designs for the U.S. Mint's Walking Liberty Half Dollar and the Winged Liberty (Mercury) Dime.

▲ **DIFFERENT FATES**

The sculpture forming the Eagle Scout Monument had stood over the east entrance of Pennsylvania Station. The other matching entrance sculptures did not fare so well. While the eagles all found perches, pieces of *Night* and *Day* were retrieved in the 1990s from a landfill and await a permanent home.

THE PENNSYLVANIA RAILROAD COMPANY PRESENTED THIS STATUARY TO THE KANSAS CITY AREA COUNCIL, BOY SCOUTS OF AMERICA, IN RECOGNITION OF SCOUTING'S CONTRIBUTION TO THIS NATION AND AS A LASTING TRIBUTE TO THOSE WHO HAVE EARNED ITS HIGHEST AWARD

THE EAGLE SCOUT BADGE

DESIGNED BY ADOLPH ALEXANDER WEINMAN, THIS ENTABLATURE GRACED THE EAST CONCOURSE ENTRANCE TO THE PENNSYLVANIA RAILROAD STATION IN NEW YORK CITY. IN 1967, AS THAT WORLD-FAMOUS LANDMARK WAS RAZED, THIS STATUARY WAS GIVEN IN RECOGNITION OF PAST ACHIEVEMENTS AND AS A CHALLENGE TO FUTURE GENERATIONS OF BOY SCOUTS

DEDICATED OCTOBER 6, 1968

The Knights of Dunamis

Between 1911 and 1925, membership in the Boy Scouts of America mushroomed from approximately 61,500 Scouts to 756,857—a twelvefold increase. It would have grown even faster if more qualified leaders had stepped forward. Unfortunately, there were few programs in place to hold the interest of older Scouts. Many Scouts earned the Eagle Scout Award and then disappeared from the program.

In 1925, 10 California Eagle Scouts set out to reverse this trend. On April 19, they met in the office of Raymond O. Hanson, Scout executive of the San Francisco Council, to form an association that would retain the interest of Eagle Scouts, uphold the dignity of the Eagle Scout Award, and provide a base for continuing leadership in the Scouting movement.

Drawing on chivalric traditions, they called their association the Knights of Dunamis. (Pronounced "DOO-na-mis," the word comes from a Greek word meaning "power" or "spirit.") The group's emblem consisted of an eagle perched on a sword resting on a shield. The sword was the sword of Sir Galahad, said to be the greatest of all knights. The shield's triangular shape signified the three parts of the Scout Oath—duty to God and country, duty to others, and duty to self.

The Knights of Dunamis was a great success in San Francisco, with a high percentage of members continuing their interest in Scouting. This success didn't go unnoticed. Within a year, the neighboring San Mateo County Council organized its own chapter, followed shortly thereafter by the Atlantic City Council. On December 14, 1929, delegates from six chapters met in San Francisco to organize a national board.

The Knights of Dunamis eventually boasted 110 chapters across the country, but this number had shrunk to 37 by 1971. In its later decades, the group became more inwardly focused, more caught up in ceremonies and degrees of knighthood than in service to Scouting. Older members enjoyed the Knights' traditions and rituals, while younger members felt torn between their obligations to the order and to their own Scout units. Drastic change was clearly needed for the group to survive.

▲ **CHAPTERS AND CHANGES**
By 1929, when this rare chapter photograph was taken, the Knights of Dunamis had grown to 13 chapters. By 1933, it had more than doubled to 27 chapters in communities across the country. Over time the group shed its secret-society trappings to more closely resemble a service fraternity. That wasn't enough, however, to stop its gradual decline and demise.

Blazer Patch

Neckerchief Slide

Early Felt Patch

Conference Delegate Badge

Lapel Pin

Decal

Ring

Felt Hat

Armband

PATCHES, PINS, AND MORE ▲

Like other parts of Scouting, the Knights of Dunamis created a variety
of items for uniform wear, including neckerchiefs, neckerchief slides,
and ribbon pins designed to hang from the button on the uniform shirt.
Other items included the hats and badges members wore to the national
conferences that began in 1929. Although rare, Knights memorabilia
occasionally crops up on auction sites like eBay.

NESA History

NESA Emblem

In August 1970, the National Chapter of the Knights of Dunamis, Inc., empowered its officers to take action to dissolve the corporation and consummate a merger with the Boy Scouts of America. In May 1971, BSA and Knights of Dunamis representatives met to plan a new organization of Eagle Scouts that would incorporate the best traditions of the Knights and of other local Eagle Scout associations around the country. In May 1972, the National Eagle Scout Association was born.

Key leaders in the creation of NESA were two members of the BSA's National Executive Board, Donald H. Flanders and J. Kimball Whitney, and the eight-year president of the Knights, Dr. Lester R. Steig. A San Francisco school administrator, Steig had long worked to revitalize the group and smooth its transition from secret society to modern association. In 1976, NESA's *Eagletter* reported that "Les Steig, probably more than any other single individual, provided the impetus for the birth of the National Eagle Scout Association."

One of NESA's first actions was to launch a vigorous membership drive at both the 1973 National Scout Jamboree and the 1973 National Order of the Arrow Conference. That same year, the organization created the NESA Scoutmaster Award to recognize the noteworthy promotion of, and leadership to, the Scouting advancement program in general and exemplary development of Eagles in particular. (The award was replaced by the Scoutmaster Award of Merit, now called the Unit Leader Award of Merit, in 1978.)

In 1978, NESA instituted its life membership program. The first life membership went to Zenon C. R. Hansen, who had been involved in Scouting for 55 years. Six years later, another key NESA effort, its scholarship program, began.

Much has changed since 1925, when ten young Eagle Scouts joined together to form the Knights of Dunamis. But one thing remains the same: NESA's commitment to retain the interest of Eagle Scouts, uphold the dignity of the Eagle Scout Award, and provide a base for continuing leadership in the Scouting movement. The objective of NESA is to serve—to serve Eagle Scouts and, through them, the entire movement of Scouting.

100 YEARS OF EAGLE SCOUTS ▶
Unveiled at the BSA's 2012 National Annual Meeting, Joseph Csatari's *100 Years of Eagle Scouts* vividly illustrates what it means to be an Eagle Scout. "He's reached the summit, and now he's ready to climb some more mountains," Csatari said. As he often does, the artist used an actual Scout as a model—in this case Matthew Dobromilsky of Troop 54 in Jamesburg, N.J., who became an Eagle Scout in 2011.

◀ **ONE HUNDRED AND COUNTING**
NESA's celebration of its own 30th birthday in 2012 understandably took a back seat to its celebration of the 100th anniversary of the Eagle Scout Award. To mark the occasion, NESA commissioned the Joseph Csatari painting *100 Years of Eagle Scouts*, introduced the commemorative patch shown here, and published an album called *100 Years of Eagle Scouts—Where Are They Now?* in conjunction with Harris Connect.

Supporting Local Councils

During the 1970s, NESA encouraged the development of local chapters, much as its predecessor, the Knights of Dunamis, had. Chapters came together at biennial national conferences, the first of which was held in Fort Collins, Colorado, in 1974.

By the mid-1980s, however, NESA had sharpened its focus on encouraging Eagle Scouts to support their local councils, not to get involved in an ancillary organization. National conferences were replaced by events at BSA annual meetings; NESA chapters gave way to council NESA committees.

As Scouting's second century began, NESA redoubled its efforts to encourage and support council NESA committees. Each issue of *Eagle Scout Magazine* profiles a committee, and the NESA office provides extensive resources to councils that want to create committees.

Today, these committees help carry out NESA's goal of identifying and involving adult Eagle Scouts. They also provide recognition to new Eagle Scouts and encourage them to enroll in NESA and stay involved in Scouting.

Each committee is charged with supporting the council's mission and vision, helping the council achieve its goals in the Journey to Excellence performance-recognition program, and finding Eagle Scouts and encouraging them to become active resources for the council's leadership and programs.

Some do even more. The committee in the Chicago Area Council holds networking events to connect Eagle Scouts working in specific industries. The committee in the Utah National Parks Council (Provo, Utah) has created Eagle Scout service clubs on local college campuses. The committee in the Dan Beard Council (Cincinnati, Ohio) provides mentors for a program that brings inner-city kids to Scout camp for a week. The committee in the Central Florida Council (Orlando) presents James E. West Fellowships to local Eagle Scouts with top service projects.

CENTRAL FLORIDA COUNCIL ▶
Headquartered in Orlando, the Central Florida Council presents James E. West Fellowship Awards to local Scouts who complete the 10 best Eagle Scout projects each year.

◀ **UTAH NATIONAL PARKS COUNCIL**
An estimated 39,000 Eagle Scouts live in the Orem-based Utah National Parks Council. The council's Eagle's Nest group uses email and LinkedIn to keep them informed.

DAN BEARD COUNCIL ▶
Each summer, the Cincinnati-based Dan Beard Council invites Eagle Scouts to visit Camp Friedlander for a steak dinner, fellowship, and the chance to tour the camp while it's in session.

◀ **MANY GENERATIONS**
Gatherings of Eagle Scouts, like this 2011 event in Cincinnati, bring together newly minted Eagle Scouts with men who are old enough to be their fathers, grandfathers, or even great-grandfathers. Divided by age, these men are nevertheless united by common experiences like hiking in the rain, cooking over open fires, serving in their communities, learning to lead their peers, and, of course, earning Scouting's highest rank.

DESA and NOESA Awards

While the Eagle Scout Award is no guarantor of success in later life, Eagle Scouts are well represented among America's leaders in business, government, education, and military and community service. Since 1912, when the first award was presented, countless Eagle Scouts have distinguished themselves in service to their communities, our nation, and the world.

In 1969, the Boy Scouts of America created the Distinguished Eagle Scout Award to recognize adult Eagle Scouts whose service has been especially noteworthy. One of the BSA's distinguished service awards (along with the Silver Beaver, Silver Antelope, Silver Buffalo, and Silver World awards), the award is unique in that it depends on the recipient's involvement in Scouting as a youth.

Youth involvement is just the beginning, however. To be considered for the award, a recipient must have distinguished himself in his profession and in community service for at least 25 years since becoming an Eagle Scout. Although adult involvement in Scouting is not a requirement, many Distinguished Eagle Scouts continue to serve actively in the program.

Nominations for the Distinguished Eagle Scout Award begin in the local council where the nominee lives. A selection sub-committee of the National Eagle Scout Association national committee must then review and approve the nomination.

Distinguished Eagle Scouts receive a gold eagle (similar to the silver eagle on the Eagle Scout medal)

that is suspended from a red, white, and blue ribbon. Those who are active in Scouting also wear a small gold eagle device on the Eagle Scout square knot on their Scout uniforms.

Because the Distinguished Eagle Scout Award recognizes accomplishment at the national level, it must exclude many Eagle Scouts who've made a mark on their local communities. To fill that void, NESA introduced the NESA Outstanding Eagle Scout Award in 2011. Approved by local council NESA committees, the award recognizes outstanding achievement at the local, state, or regional level; recognition items include a neck medal featuring an eagle in flight suspended from a blue ribbon studded with fleurs-de-lys.

NESA OUTSTANDING EAGLE SCOUT AWARD ▶
Introduced in 2011, the NESA Outstanding Eagle Scout Award lets councils honor Eagle Scouts who have consistently given back to their communities. The number of NOESAs a local council can present each year is based on its number of new Eagle Scouts.

DISTINGUISHED EAGLE SCOUT AWARD ▶
Since its establishment in 1969, the Distinguished Eagle Scout Award has gained prominent standing among Scouting recognitions. Recipients have included President Gerald R. Ford, governors and senators, military flag officers, university presidents, leaders of Fortune 500 companies, and nationally known lawyers, educators, and doctors.

◀ **THOMAS R. NORRIS**
NESA Director Bill Steele and NESA President Glenn Adams presented the Distinguished Eagle Scout Award to Medal of Honor recipient Thomas Norris on October 24, 2011. Lt. Norris, who was grievously wounded in Vietnam, went on to serve in the FBI for two decades. More recently, he has joined other Medal of Honor recipients in urging today's veterans to seek help in adjusting to life after combat.

▲ **MATTHEW S. HOLLAND**
On March 28, 2011, the Utah National Parks Council presented the NESA Outstanding Eagle Scout Award to Matthew Holland, PhD, president of Utah Valley University. A political scientist by training, Dr. Holland has received national attention for his research on how ideals of Christian charity influenced the development of American political life. Standing with Dr. Holland are NESA Regent Dr. William A. Miller and Professor Marty Val Hill, Chairman of the Utah National Parks Council NESA Committee.

131

The Adams Award

Developed and funded by NESA President Glenn Adams and his wife in 2010, the Glenn A. and Melinda W. Adams National Eagle Scout Service Project of the Year Award does just what its name implies: honors America's best Eagle project each year.

That's a tall order, considering that more than 50,000 Scouts complete Eagle projects annually. Every week, in fact, several hundred Eagle Scout candidates are at work on projects in their local communities or in locations around the world.

To qualify for the Adams Award, a Scout must submit his project to his local council's NESA committee for consideration during January of the year after he passed his Eagle Scout board of review. (His project does not have to have taken place during the same year.) The council forwards its top project to the regional NESA committee. Four regional winners are selected in March, and a single national winner is selected in April. The award is then presented in May or June during the NESA Americanism Breakfast at the BSA's National Annual Meeting.

The national winner receives a plaque, a silver device for his Eagle Scout square knot, and a scholarship of $2,500. The three regional winners who don't win the national award receive a framed certificate, a gold device for their Eagle Scout square knots, and a $500 educational or Scouting scholarship. Council winners receive a framed certificate and a bronze device for their Eagle Scout square knots. Their names also appear on a permanent plaque located in their council service center or camp.

ALEX GRIFFITH ▲

People from all over the world have responded to Alex's story. "I have received letters and emails from Scouts who now are planning bigger and more meaningful projects and from adopted kids who now want to go back and do something for their communities," Alex said.

JEFF COX

When he set out to build a 9/11 memorial in Windermere, Florida, as his Eagle Scout project, Jeff Cox knew he wanted it to be about more than just America. "I wanted to incorporate the international loss of life," he said. "What people don't realize is that there were a lot of people from other countries that also had sufferings and loss." To that end, he created tiles representing each country that lost citizens on 9/11, along with tiles for police and fire departments and the Pentagon.

▲ A GREAT CELEBRATION

More than 1,300 people attended the dedication of Jeff Cox's 9/11 memorial, including several family members of those who died in the terrorist attacks. "I actually hang out with a few of them," Jeff said. "For a few of them, it's really helped bring closure."

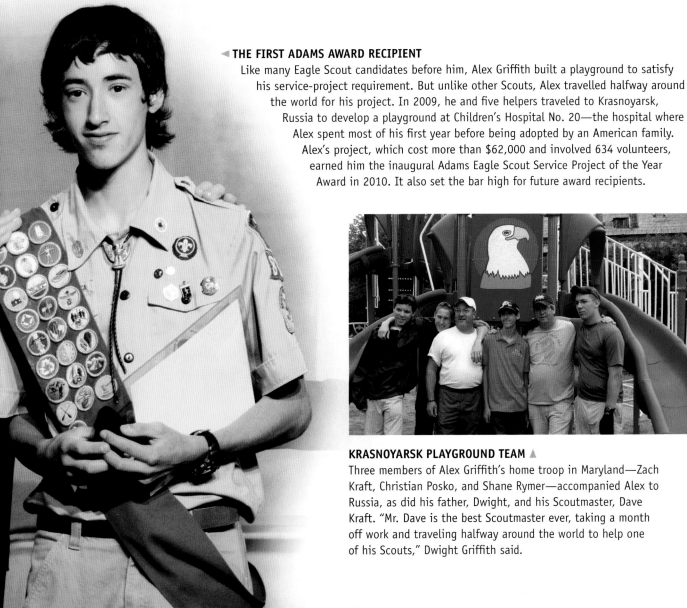

◄ THE FIRST ADAMS AWARD RECIPIENT

Like many Eagle Scout candidates before him, Alex Griffith built a playground to satisfy his service-project requirement. But unlike other Scouts, Alex travelled halfway around the world for his project. In 2009, he and five helpers traveled to Krasnoyarsk, Russia to develop a playground at Children's Hospital No. 20—the hospital where Alex spent most of his first year before being adopted by an American family. Alex's project, which cost more than $62,000 and involved 634 volunteers, earned him the inaugural Adams Eagle Scout Service Project of the Year Award in 2010. It also set the bar high for future award recipients.

KRASNOYARSK PLAYGROUND TEAM ▲

Three members of Alex Griffith's home troop in Maryland—Zach Kraft, Christian Posko, and Shane Rymer—accompanied Alex to Russia, as did his father, Dwight, and his Scoutmaster, Dave Kraft. "Mr. Dave is the best Scoutmaster ever, taking a month off work and traveling halfway around the world to help one of his Scouts," Dwight Griffith said.

NESA at National Events

A total of 43,434 Scouts and leaders attended the 2010 National Scout Jamboree. At times, it appeared that all of them were trying to crowd into the NESA tent on Thomas Road.

Why all the traffic? Many visitors came to have their pictures taken with a bald eagle from the National Eagle Center in Wabasha, Minnesota. Others wanted to check out Terry Grove's comprehensive collection of Eagle Scout medals and patches. Still others wanted to rub shoulders with some of the nationally prominent Eagle Scouts who visited the tent each day.

NESA maintains a presence like that at every national jamboree, using the event as a chance to promote the organization and to encourage Scouts to become Eagle Scouts. The organization is also visible at the BSA's National Annual Meeting, where its popular Americanism Breakfast draws upwards of 1,400 guests to celebrate America and the accomplishments of Eagle Scouts.

PASSING THE TORCH ▲
At the 2010 National Scout Jamboree, NESA volunteer Tony DiSalvo, a 1945 Eagle Scout, distributed commemorative pins to Scouts as they marched toward the opening arena show.

COLONEL CHARLES MCGEE ▼
At the 2010 National Scout Jamboree, NESA presented the Distinguished Eagle Scout Award to Col. McGee, one of the original Tuskegee Airman. On hand for the ceremony were 51 Distinguished Eagle Scouts—roughly one out of every 20 living DESA recipients. It was the largest gathering of DESA recipients to date.

MORE THAN HOT AIR ▶
The NESA balloon appears at every national jamboree, inspiring current and future Eagle Scouts (along with visitors like these Japanese Scouts at the 2010 National Jamboree) to soar high. Eagle Scout Ralph Armstrong, a Louisiana physician and balloon enthusiast, started the BSA balloon program in the early 1980s.

Eagle Scout Testimonials

Achieving the Eagle Scout rank is an exceptional achievement for a Boy Scout, something attained by only 5 percent of all Scouts.

Many Eagles go on to achieve great things in their lives, and a handful of the more famous Eagle alumni are celebrated in Chapter 5 of this book. But in the Centennial of the first Eagle Scout Award, we were also keen to celebrate less well-known Eagles, and fascinated to know how achieving this rank had influenced their lives—both at the time and in later life.

Through our social media channels, we asked the question: "If you're an Eagle Scout, tell us what it means to you and how it has influenced your life, or perhaps share a favorite memory of your Trail to Eagle."

We received a large number of responses, all of them testifying to the huge impact that achieving Eagle Scout had made to people's lives. The following represents just a few of the many personal stories submitted by Eagle Scouts—of all ages and from every walk of life.

John T. Dressler

Eagle Scout: 1961 **Troop:** 225, Lucedale, MS

The Scouts taught me lessons and values I may have missed due to growing up without a father. It was the most stable part of my childhood.

"Be Prepared," that is what I have lived by. I became a scout when I was 11 years old in Biloxi, Mississippi. My Scoutmaster was Mr. Charlie Hart of Troop 25. While I lived in Biloxi, I became a Life Scout. Then, in January 1961, my mother and I were in an auto accident and she was killed. My father had died in 1946, two months before my birth, so I went to live with my grandparents in Lucedale, Mississippi. When I came to Lucedale, I joined Troop 225 and earned my Eagle Scout Award in the spring of 1961. When my troop went to the Boy Scout jamboree in Colorado I was an Eagle Scout. I paid my way in full by cutting grass, and while I was there I shook the hand of Dwight D. Eisenhower, president of the United States. The Scouts taught me lessons and values I may have missed due to growing up without a father. It was the most stable part of my childhood.

Steven Chait

Eagle Scout: 1982 **Troop:** 70, Springfield, NJ

What does it mean to be an Eagle Scout? Recently, my wife asked me the same question as I went off to a job interview.

I became an Eagle in 1982. My board of review was on the night before I turned 18. Our troop was a very unique group of individuals, from all walks of life. The knowledge and skills we now possess are unmatched. I use the Scout Oath and Law every day and try to instill them in the people I encounter, which includes the boys in my troop.

Dean S. Grason

Eagle Scout: 1984 **Troop:** 199, Redwood City, CA

Growing up, I was always the smallest kid and the last to be picked for a team. I was even cut one year by the coach of my elementary school's flag football team because he was afraid I might get hurt.

Scouts offered me an opportunity to excel. Regardless of my height, I was given the chance to succeed, whether it was building a monkey bridge, backpacking 100 miles at age 12, being a patrol leader at a national jamboree at age 13, or earning merit badges and ranks along my Trail to Eagle. I was no longer the short kid; I was the patrol leader, senior patrol leader, or OA district chief. I felt I could achieve any goal I set my mind to.

As an older teen, I thought that was the only lesson I learned, but as an adult I realized that the skills I learned as a Scout were applicable to everyday life. Now, as an adult with kids, I find that my sons are inspired by being Scouts, and have a desire to achieve Eagle themselves and become the next generation of leaders.

I didn't realize how deeply Scouting had influenced my life until my oldest son told me how good he feels when his grandma takes him to the park and he sits on the benches I built as part of my Eagle project, almost 30 years ago.

Scott Holmes

Eagle Scout: 2011 **Troop:** 119, Deerfield Beach, FL

Ever since I was in Cub Scouts, I would attend the Eagle ceremonies of older Scouts in our troop and was just mesmerized.

Throughout my Scouting career I knew I was going to get my Eagle before turning 18. I pictured myself standing up in front of my friends and family while reciting the Eagle Scout Oath, thinking who I would thank during my Eagle response. I know the amount of responsibility that rank holds in society, and I always get praises when I tell people that I am an Eagle Scout.

Being an Eagle Scout means living the Scout Oath and Law at all times. With only 5 percent of Boy Scouts earning the Eagle rank, I feel proud to be part of this distinguished group of men.

Greg Every

Eagle Scout: 1978 **Troop:** 400, Livonia, MI

Well, let's start with my first job as a teen. I told the boss at the end of an uneventful interview, "By the way I just earned my Eagle Scout Award last month." He responded with, "When can you start?" That was when I realized that my Eagle Scout Award really is a big deal.

When I started a business in my twenties, I learned that by living the Scout Law, others will respect and trust you. Just by being honest about a deal that a large company made a mistake on, I was extended credit. I built on this attitude and continue to use it every day in my business. This, and staying physically strong, morally straight, and mentally awake, has given me a great marriage and a great sports business in Detroit.

I have two sons that are active in Scouting, and I tell them all the time how important Scouting is.

Bill Dundulis III

Eagle Scout: 2004, **Troop:** 2, Woonsocket, RI

During the Eagle ceremony in my troop, part of the Eagle charge includes calling the candidate a "marked man." Your actions are known whether you're wearing the uniform or not, and that being an Eagle is for life.

When things look bad, the first person to give up is usually you. I wanted to give up Scouting but didn't because my father, William Dundulis Jr, and my Scoutmaster, Earl Minot, never let me. I didn't know it at the time, but later I knew they were right. The two of them were important anchors in my life and I don't think I would be the man I am today without them.

The resilience I have learned as an Eagle has really helped me. A few years ago, when I became ill with a lung infection, every day was a struggle. My doctor told me that he had seen patients over the years with less serious problems who had fought him every inch, but I never complained and never gave up. I eventually got better and became very active in my council, teaching Scouts what I have learned. I now serve as a unit commissioner for three units in Blackstone, MA.

Ben Luedloff

Eagle Scout: 2007 **Troop:** 603, Wildwood, MO

I want the BSA to continue to instill its values in the young men and women of our nation. It's no secret that Scouting forms our country's great leaders; to have even a small role in making the experience even better would mean the world to me.

Serving on my local council's camp staff, gazing out upon the beautiful mountains at Philmont, and being elected as an Order of the Arrow lodge chief—Scouting provided me with these experiences and so much more, and the memories will never fade.

The Scout Oath and Law aren't simply words to an Eagle Scout; they carry a profound meaning and challenge.

The Scout Oath and Law aren't simply words to an Eagle Scout; they carry a profound meaning and challenge. If you know me, you know that I have an unlimited passion for the Boy Scouts of America. The BSA has been a significant part of my life over the past 14 years. I have met countless people in the program, made lifelong friends, and influenced young men while serving on camp staff—and I've loved every minute of it.

My journey to Eagle began as a Tiger Cub. I wanted to belong and wear the uniform that the "big kids" wore in Cub Scouts. Scouting was a place where I could spend time outdoors with my friends. Today, as an Eagle Scout and assistant Scoutmaster, nothing feels more gratifying than sharing my love of Scouting with the next generation of young men. My passion for the Boy Scouts of America has inspired me to pursue a career in professional Scouting.

Brian Woznicki

Eagle Scout: 1971 **Troop:** 652, Rosemont, PA

Earning Eagle still has a big spot among my personal memories; not only as an accomplishment but as a paradigm for learning, service, and fun.

Saturday, May 15, 1971 is unlikely to make the annals of history, but it will always have enormous significance to me. That is the day when I received my Eagle Scout Award—the culmination of over six years of working, playing, learning, and planning.

At the time, 21 merit badges were needed to earn Eagle; 11 required and 10 elective. Two of the required merit badges were Swimming and Life Saving, but because I have cerebral palsy I could not meet the requirements for either. However, the BSA has a provision that permits a Scout who is unable to earn required merit badges due to disability to substitute other badges. Our local council put a rider on this provision, requiring a Scout to

earn two merit badges for every one badge he was unable to earn. This seemed unfair, but I went with it.

Another major requirement for earning Eagle Scout is performing a 50-hour community service project. The textbook projects, such as registering people to vote or clearing litter from highways, couldn't work for me. My service project literally moved in next door—a family of four from France. The two young girls in the family enrolled in the local parish school, but spoke very little English and needed help with their home work. My mom and I helped them one hour every day after school. They were bright and motivated. Every homework session ended with a snack.

This was the last major hurdle and I breezed through the required paper work. The last step was the board of review, about a 45-minute interview with a panel of six Scout leaders and one Scout who had already earned Eagle. It was 45 minutes of sweaty palms, but it was conducted in a somewhat relaxed manner. I passed, and the story of my accomplishment reached the local media and the international press. One public relations professional even wanted to work on endorsement contracts. Imagine that! For a 17-year-old kid from the Philadelphia suburbs it was a huge deal. Earning Eagle still has a big spot among my personal memories; not only as an accomplishment but as a paradigm for learning, service, and fun.

Charles McCombs

Eagle Scout: 2010, **Troop:** 332, Worthington, OH

Being an Eagle Scout is more than just a rank, it is a lifestyle.

Being an Eagle Scout is more than just a rank, it is a lifestyle. I have learned so much from Scouts that no matter the situation, I am always prepared.

My journey to Eagle has proved so influential that I even picked my career path based on the values and skills I learned as a Scout. The first aid training I received, and the desire to help people that has been instilled in me, are the reasons that I am currently studying to become a doctor. I believe that as a doctor I will be in a great position to live out the ideals of an Eagle Scout by helping people when they are in need, and providing service to the community that I live in. My journey to Eagle taught me how important this is.

Aidan Judd

Eagle Scout: 2010, **Troop:** 351, Wrightwood, CA

For my Eagle project, my fellow Scouts and I conducted video interviews with veterans from our local Veterans of Foreign Wars. Their experiences and memories spanned from World War II to Desert Storm, from Bastogne to Baghdad. I raised the money to purchase a kiosk system to archive those memories in a touch screen computer. The archive is organized by name, by war, and by branch of service.

In the year since the original 21 interviews, I have continued to record veterans' memories. We often don't realize how many of those around us are veterans who have compelling stories to share. I'm amazed by the connections I have made, not only with the veterans but with their families as well. Many vets' wives have said, "He told you more in 20 minutes than he's told me in 20 years!"

Recently, when Vietnam vet, "Big Al" died, his family invited me to his wake at the VFW, and thanked me for what the Scouts had done to keep his stories alive. I was surprised and touched to see that they had his video interview running continuously in the background for his loved ones to watch. His brother came up to me to say that his whole family owed me a debt of gratitude. I learned a lot from my project, but the most important thing I learned is that as these wars slide into history, we need to keep the flame of patriotism alive.

Richard Smith

Eagle Scout: 1970 **Troop:** 461, Durham, NC

For me, it was about our Scout master, Charles "Chuck" Brackett. Mr. "B" was a veteran of the beaches of Iwo Jima. Man, was he skilled: he taught us how to handle a hatchet, how to steer a boat, how to tell the truth. Troop meetings started in formation, and all of us had to put our hands out for finger nail inspection. No nail biting in Troop 461. A lie didn't wash because the nails told the tale. He also showed how to make things, like pontoon boats, and blackberry pie using Wonder Bread.

We were kids from all walks of life—sons of gas station owners or professors. On one camping trip, we were chased around a Saturday evening bonfire by Bigfoot! We had shouted into the hills of the Piedmont: "Spirit of land, spirit of darkness, spirit of sea, send Bigfoot to me." Later, we found out it was Mr. B's buddy dressed up in a gorilla outfit. Just once he let me fire his 45 into an old pine tree. Talk about a kick. After the World War II, he was stationed in Japan and came to love the Japanese people. There was a lesson in this too.

Andrew Decker

Eagle Scout: 2012, **Troop:** 904, Webb City, MO

Doing my Eagle Scout project made me realize that people are always willing to help others who have suffered badly. I felt privileged to be part of that.

My favorite memory along my Trail to Eagle was my Eagle Scout project. I love music, and play the saxophone in my high school marching band and jazz band. I live about six miles from where an EF5 tornado ripped through Joplin, Missouri, on May 22, 2011. At that time, I was looking for a project to do and decided on an instrument drive for those students who had lost their instruments as a result of the tornado.

At first, I was a little worried that people would not be able to donate such expensive items. My aim was to try and collect 20 instruments. More students than that were affected but I figured it would be a good start. I enlisted the help of a couple of news reporters who interviewed me to get the word out to the public. I also received help from the local YMCA, which provided drop-off points for people wishing to donate instruments. I spent many hours on this project, and in the end I collected over 70 instruments.

The whole experience was very rewarding experience and one that I will never forget. I was so grateful for the opportunity to bring some normality and comfort to some of those affected by the tornado. Doing my Eagle Scout project made me realize that people are always willing to help others who have suffered badly. I felt privileged to be part of that.

Adam Seab

Eagle Scout: 1996 **Troop:** 220, Moss Point, MS

My time in the Boy Scouts was an enjoyable time in my life. I made many friends that, 16 years later, I still talk to. Scouting is a great opportunity for kids who may not get any other chance to enjoy the outdoors to acquire important life skills.

I believe that now more than ever, kids need a program that can give guidance and provide positive mentors who are able to teach them how to be responsible, learn to love their country, and get involved in their community.

Being an Eagle Scout helped my career by proving to me that I could accomplish something that I started, and could be trusted and depended on. I'm glad that Scouting is still going strong, and I look forward to the time when I can get my son involved in the program.

Kyle Zulfer

Eagle Scout: 2008 **Troop:** 501, Spruce Pine, NC

To me being an Eagle Scout is everything. My name is Kyle Zulfer. I am an Eagle Scout from Troop 501, based in Spruce Pine, North Carolina. Growing up in a small town I had fewer opportunities than most, but because of Scouting I had more than I would have ever dreamed.

The road to Eagle is not an easy one to follow, and there are a lot of ups and downs, but in the end you can look back at the journey and say: "look at what I have done!" Because of my Eagle rank I received my first job with no problem. My boss later explained to me why he chose me over other more qualified applicants; he told me, "I choose you because I know how hard it is to achieve the rank of Eagle, and it shows me that you will stick with this job and not give up."

Putting Eagle Scout on my college application resulted in me being part of the first round picks for the incoming year. It also helped in receiving over $20,000 in scholarships which, trust me, helps out a lot. Being an Eagle Scout was one of the biggest journeys in my life, but it was well worth the effort.

Index

Boy Scouts of America®

The mission of the Boy Scouts of America is to prepare young people to make ethical and moral choices over their lifetimes by instilling in them the values of the Scout Oath and Scout Law. The programs of the Boy Scouts of America—Cub Scouting, Boy Scouting, Varsity Scouting, and Venturing®—pursue these aims through methods designed for the age and maturity of the participants.

Cub Scouting

Fun with a purpose, Cub Scouting is an activity-filled, quality experience for boys 7 to 10 years old (first grade through fifth grade). Adult family members are encouraged to play a strong supportive role in their Cub Scout's success. Tiger Cubs are first-graders. Webelos are fourth- and fifth-graders getting ready to cross over into Boy Scout troops. Cub Scouting helps all its members grow into good citizens who are strong in character and personally fit.

Boy Scouting

Based on the values of the Scout Oath and Scout Law, Boy Scouting is for boys ages 11 through 17. (Boys may also become Boy Scouts if they have earned the Webelos Arrow of Light Award or have completed the fifth grade.) With outdoor adventures, leadership, service to others, and achievement through rank advancement, Boy Scouting's vigorous program achieves the BSA's objectives of developing character, citizenship, and personal fitness.

Varsity Scouting

An active, exciting program for young men ages 14 through 17, Varsity Scouting is built around five fields of emphasis: advancement, high adventure, personal development, service, and special programs and events.

Venturing®

The BSA's opportunity for women and men ages 13 through 20 years of age, Venturing® includes challenging high-adventure activities, sports, leadership, service, and career exploration as ways for young people to mature into responsible, caring adults. (Sea Scouting is a segment of Venturing® that promotes maritime skills and heritage.)

For more information about the Boy Scouts of America or its programs, visit www.scouting.org

Picture Credits

The publisher would like to thank the **Boy Scouts of America** and the **National Eagle Scout Association** for permission to reproduce their photographs. The following were provided by the **National Scouting Museum**: 4–5b, 6l, 7tr, 18–19, 21, 23, 24, 25tr, 25bl, 26r, 28–29, 31tr, 32, 33t, 34–35b, 37, 39, 41, 43tc, 43tr, 46l, 60–61, 63tr, 63tc, 63tl, 73tl, 76t, 76c, 76cr, 76cl, 86, 87l, 90tr, 111, 113.

Abbreviation Key
t-top, b-bottom, r-right, l-left, c-center.

Also, thanks to the following individuals and picture agencies:

Wally Berg: 85; **Robert Birkby:** 65c, 89c; **Boy Scouts of the Philippines:** 58br; **University of Chicago:** 92c; **Congressional Medal of Honor Society:** 74; **Corbis:** Theo Westenberger 102bl; Wang Shen/Xinhua Press 103; Thierry Boccon-Gibod/Pool/Reuters 105; Doug Wilson 107b; Rick Friedman 95; Sean Gardner/Reuters 97; **Dr. Dennis Crockett:** 116b, 117tl, 117b; **Joseph Csatari:** 125; **Dan Beard Council:** 126–127b; **DK Images:** 94–95cb; **Henry Doktorski:** 96cl, 96br; **David Eby:** 122, 123tr, 123cr, 123bl; **Evangeline Area Council, BSA:** 112t; **Getty Images:** Hunter Martin 98–99; Tony Duffy 99; Paul J. Richards/AFP Photo 100; Ronald C. Modra/Sports Imagery 100–101; FPG 118bl; **Dr. Terry Grove:** 46–49, 54; **Carl Imhoff:** 82–83; **Doug Keppler:** 40br; **Korea Scout Association:** 59tl; **Daniel F. Machado:** 123tl, 123tc, 123cl, 123c, 123br; **Marriott:** 106c, 106cr; **Burke Morden:** 64, 65t, 65br; **NASA:** 6, 78–79, 90b, 91; **The Norwegian Guide and Scout Association:** 59bl; **Scott Parazynski:** 84bl, 84br; **Bobbi Robinson:** 119; **Scouts Australia:** 59tc; **Scouts Canada:** 59tr; **Scouting Ireland:** 59br; **Eric Simonson:** 84tr; **South African Scout Association:** 59bc; **Stange Company:** 50–51; **Keith Weller for Johns Hopkins Medicine:** 92bl; **Clay Wood:** 53; The photographs on 94tr are from *Naturalist* by E.O. Wilson. Copyright © 1994 Island Press, Illustrations © 1994 Laura Simonds Southworth. Reproduced by permission of Island Press, Washington, DC; Images reproduced by permission of The Scout Association (UK): 58bl, 58bc, 58cl.

Every effort has been made to trace the copyright holders, and the publisher apologizes in advance for any unintentional omissions. We will be pleased to insert the appropriate acknowledgment in any subsequent edition of this publication.

Acknowledgements

Author Acknowledgements: James E. Atkinson; Wally Berg; Dr. Dennis Crockett; Carl Imhoff; Larry Johnson; Ryan Larson; Ann McFerrin; the Burke Morden family; Dr. Scott Parazynski; Mark Ray; Mitch Reis; Bobbi Robinson; Eric Simonson; Phil Smart, Sr.; Marty Tschetter; Gary Twite.

A special thanks to Dr. Terry Grove for sharing his collection of Eagle Scout Awards and emblems.

Boy Scouts of America® Acknowledgments: Assembling a book the size and scope of *Eagle Scouts: A Centennial History* is a tremendous undertaking. Untold hours of research and review have been devoted to this effort, and the Boy Scouts of America would like to acknowledge the following individuals and their contributions.

Research Team: The research team worked closely with the author and publisher to assemble the historical documents for reproduction and reviewed information for accuracy.
Beth Blair, managing editor/team leader communications, BSA; Janine Halverson, senior program assistant in international, BSA; Bob Mersereau, assistant chief scout executive, BSA; Janice Babineaux, director, National Scouting Museum, BSA; Corry Kanzenberg, curator of collections and exhibits, National Scouting Museum, BSA; Steven Price, archivist, National Scouting Museum, BSA; Gail Mayfield, assistant curator of collections and exhibits, National Scouting Museum, BSA; Jim Wilson, department manager, media services and public relations, BSA; Michael Roytek, photo manager, BSA; Christy Batchelor, photo technician, BSA; Bill Steele, director, alumni relations and NESA, BSA; Jeff Laughlin, program assistant, BSA; Keith Courson, editorial account manager, BSA.

Lead Team: The lead team provided daily coordination and management of the project from initial concept to the published piece: Gillian S. Murrell, licensing specialist, business development team, BSA; David L. Harkins, associate director, business development, BSA.

Eagle Scout Testimonials: Thanks to everyone who submitted personal statements and photographs, especially to those selected for inclusion in *Eagle Scouts: A Centennial History*: John T. Dressler; Steven Chait; Dean S. Grason; Chris Kelly; Richie Benner; Matthew Parnell; Devin McArdle; Scott Holmes; Greg Every; Bill Dundulis III; Ben Luedloff; Brian Woznicki; Charles McCombs; Aidan Judd; Richard Smith; Andrew Decker; Adam Seab; Kyle Zulfer; Aron Payne; Chad Selmek; Alex Volansky; John Gelinas, Jr.; Watson L. Clark; Franklin Brown; Jordan Woika; Thomas Lynch.

From DK

DK would additionally like to thank Eric Titner for proofreading, Hilary Bird for the index, and Ros Walford for editorial assistance.

For Further Reading: *A Comprehensive Guide to the Eagle Scout Award* by Dr. Terry Grove; *A Guide to Dating and Identifying BSA Badges, Uniforms and Insignia* by Mitch Reis; *Legacy of Honor* by Alvin Townley; *100 Years of Eagle Scouts: Where Are They Now?* (NESA).